Alone
In The Wind

America As Seen From The Saddle Of A
V-Twin In The Late 1980's

Charles L Schiereck

My heart went out to the pioneer families in their wagon trains who would have been faced by the same grim prospects. Hurried along by their determination to pass Independence Rock by July 4th, here it was June and the passes were snowbound.

- ALONE IN THE WIND -

A Journal Of Discovery
In
"The Summer of 88"

Two roads diverged in a yellow wood,
And sorry I could not travel both
And be one traveler, long I stood
And looked down one as far as I could
To where it bent in the undergrowth

Robert Frost 'The Road Not Taken'

Introduction

This effort fulfills a need to unburden, to lay out the whole story with one pitch. Much of this account has been told, but never all of it, in sequence, to one listener at a time until now.

Some of what's included in the text is the result of long reflection. Having had such strong preconceptions up front as to what to expect, my mind was too often clouded, diminishing my ability to recognize what was going on around me at the time. In some cases it would take decades to untangle.

The process of exorcising this demon finally ended in the summer of 2014, at a bar in Ft Lauderdale, during halftime of the World Cup Final.

PROLOGUE

I don't always understand what motivates me, but in this case, the seed had always been there.

In February of 1985, I was lying on a bed at the Princeton Medical Center. Two spinal disks, damaged in a parachuting accident had just been removed. With my lower spine fused, recovery would be a long process.

This was the first in a string of disruptive events that would dominate the next few years of my life. I wasn't getting any younger, and the recovery, followed by a divorce and a couple of dead end relationships seemed to weigh heavily. I was by no means unhappy, and none of these events were destructive, just a normal part of getting older and dealing with life. However, when my father passed unexpectedly in 87, I knew I could choose to 'stay the course' and stagnate, or stir the pot and grow. The clock keeps ticking either way.

Restless as a kid, I always needed to know what was beyond the horizon. On the first warm days each spring, my heart would ache to be moving on. Maybe these were just the remnants of migration instincts, reminders of a distant past where a change of seasons prompted a change in location. I don't know if everyone feels these tugs; many poets such as Robert Frost certainly did, and for me the pull was becoming more urgent.

I remember dwelling on a comment made by a college friend who'd driven a bike from California back to New Jersey. Young men talk big, and I'd done my share of that - but his trip was a story that seemed to be worth hearing.

I wasn't interested in a point-to-point ride with a fixed destination. I wanted to stay flexible, follow my nose, let the wind guide me.

What followed was two years of recovery, slowly regaining strength as my imagination ran wild. It became clear that I was being presented with a chance to put up or shut up. I could seize this window of opportunity, or kiss it goodbye forever.

At some point it became clear that I *was* going to see it through. I wasn't looking for excuses to bail out; I was seeking destinations, and routes. The seed had sprouted and escape velocity would not be far behind.

On a cold April morning, I parked my car at the far eastern end of Main Street in Manasquan, then made the short hike to the waters edge. Five minutes later, my hands were numb and my feet wet, but there were two small bottles of Atlantic Ocean on the front seat.

Tower Falls - Yellowstone

1
ON THE ROAD

<u>*Journal Entry May 20th, 1988*</u>*: It's 9 pm and I'm sitting on the motorcycle in the garage, wondering what I might be forgetting. The realization that I've over packed lies several days ahead.*

Outside the open door, a steady rain continues as it has all week, drowning any hopes for a sunny departure.

Discouraged by the prospects of a major storm front stalled over the Northeast, I knew that tomorrow would also be wet. If there was one 'take away lesson' from my dry run to Watkins Glen, it was that 'riding in a downpour sucks'.

Rain was pouring down and every omen said 'WAIT', but waiting had no place in what little plan there was. I would bite down, head west and try to blow through the worst of the storms.

Sweating in the thick humid air, I leaned back in the saddle as old doubts crept into my head. All the excuses I've used in the past tempted me. Why was I bothering?

Moist air hung around the single yellow bulb in the dirty ceiling. Lethargic moths repeatedly flew into it as if to show how pointless life can be. That wasn't going to happen to me. Rain or shine, the show would start tomorrow. I'd been given a blank check, the chance to indulge a life-long wanderlust with no end in sight. My mind filled with mountains and forests, dreams of gliding down long red canyons, the evening sun low on the horizon. If anything had been forgotten, I could pick it up on the road.

Journal Entry May 21st, 1988: Five am - still dark and still raining. I went out to the garage and started the engine. Dressing quickly, all the doors and windows were checked one last time.

Back in the garage the engine was starting to warm as I scanned the sky. There was a lull in the rain, a chance to break out, and that was encouraging.

The engine roared as I accelerated the bike out onto an empty Route 57, heading west. It was only seven miles to the Pennsylvania border at Easton, but the cold quickly penetrated my jacket, requiring a quick stop to put on sweater and gloves.

Minutes later after paying the toll, I rolled over the Delaware River, obscured below me by an early morning fog. The air was colder and smelled of dampness and mud.

Sitting atop the hill to my right is Lafayette College, where as a freshman in 1968 I'd look down at the late night trucks on Route 22 and wonder where they were headed. Where had those twenty years gone?"

I'd spent three years at Lafayette, from 68 through 71 and never did graduate. That would come in 1974 with a degree from Monmouth College. Even now, I'm occasionally haunted by my failures at Lafayette, and still wonder about the cause. Vietnam and the draft was some of it. My original plan had been to attend the Coast Guard academy, but after I failed the physical due to eyesight, there was no 'Plan B'. That played a role as well - I just wasn't interested in anything else. 'No future, no interest?' .

When a position became available in the National Guard, I jumped. Was this just taking the easy way out? Should I have sucked it up and fought my way through at Lafayette instead of quitting? My parents had worked hard to get me to that point.

As I drove the highway beneath 'College Hill' that day I didn't know, still felt somewhat guilty.

Journal Entry 1988: At Carlisle I turned south on Route 34. The sun was out and I was starting to relax for the first time. This was the route in 1863 that General Richard Ewell used to lead parts of his Confederate II Corps south to disaster at Gettysburg. It was obvious that the land hadn't changed very much since then. The countryside was beautiful - Farmland and livestock, fields and flowers, the passions of late spring on a sunny morning. The air smelled of manure and turned wet earth.

In my ears, the engine rumble deepened as I throttled up to take on a hill. Five miles south of Carlisle, I passed a gathering at a rail crossing. Steam exhaust was visible through the trees and in a minute, barking and breathing fire, the engine appeared.

I considered that stumbling upon this scene so early in the trip was a fair omen. As soon as the train was past, the rail fans dashed for their cars and tried to beat the engine to the next grade crossing. Staying well clear of that mob, I kept rolling. With engine pounding and a hot sun in my face, my nose was pointing south.

Just short of Gettysburg the engine coughed; I reached down with my left hand and switched the fuel petcock to "RESERVE". There was a surge as the engine roared back to life; but it was time to fill up and check the maps.

2
GETTYSBURG

The good stuff is west of the Mississippi and I'm hell bent for the Bridges.

Gettysburg was an exception. So close, it seemed absurd that I'd never made the effort to visit. Storms were on the horizon and I had little time to lose, but I was going to squeeze this stop in.

The town was crowded and I quickly headed west, then parked and explored the Lutheran seminary grounds. Here Union forces made their final stand on the first day of fighting before retreating back to Cemetery Ridge.

Time never stands still, everything changes, but not so much at Gettysburg.

The Park Service has done a fine job of keeping the battlefields true.

I invested two hours visiting the sites of major engagements and it could just as easily have been two weeks. The Peach Orchard, Wheat Field, Devils Den, and the Round Tops got quick service, followed by a slow cruise along Cemetery Ridge. West out of town, I repeated the 'drive by' along the old Confederate lines.

A student of this campaign for many years, I'm well sick of the ceaseless bickering that goes on to this day over every aspect of the battle. Even 'soft' experts today wield their opinions like swords. They know more of the battle's comings and goings than anyone alive at the time did. Still, the girl who cringed in the basement for four days, then lived with the smell for the rest of the summer, had a much clearer idea of what really happened than any of the 'experts' today.

I've heard that on dark nights you can smell blood down in 'Devil's Den'. That day in the sunshine, kids were playing among the boulders and I wondered for a moment if this was disrespectful. My head cleared, life moves on, let the kids play.

Moving South-West out of Gettysburg on the old Hagerstown pike, roughly paralleling the Confederate retreat of July 4th 1863, I reconsidered my options.

Journal Entry 1988: The sun was shining, but storm clouds darkened the horizons. One way or another, I was in for heavy weather and it might have been better to pass on Gettysburg and keep rolling. After crossing the Maryland border I pulled onto I-81 Southbound. I'd planned to cruise the Shenandoah Valley on back roads, but now, expecting storms, the Interstate seems safer.

As thunder heads began to loom in the distance, I

wasn't so sure – there was no place to hide on the interstate. What began as a beautiful afternoon ride through scenic countryside, looked to end as a cold, wet test of endurance. Maryland was gone in the blink of an eye. At a rest stop in West Virginia a bus driver assured me that "there's bad shit ahead". I was getting tired and sore but kept pushing south.

Well into Virginia the storms advanced, rolling down the road in the gloom. Occasional rumbles, felt rather than heard over the engine, became more frequent. Soon the middle distance was veiled by a grey curtain that seemed to solidify as I got closer. I could see the rain hitting the road a quarter mile ahead, then suddenly, I was in it.

I'd watched this storm come on for ten minutes, but the transition was startling nonetheless - more because of the quick temperature change than the downpour.

Slowing to forty, I stayed to the right and kept one eye glued to the mirrors. I left the rain gear in the bags and stayed with leathers. Earlier, the "brain bucket" had been swapped out for the full face helmet and that was a good move. Visibility was bad. The rain-streaked visor was lifted a bit so I could snatch glimpses of the road at quick intervals. I'd have loved to tuck behind a car and let them figure out where the road was, but there were none to be seen.

Instantaneous thunderclaps followed the hot bolts of lightning and there was no preparing for them. I kept moving. A few more lightening strikes and the road ahead appeared to brighten a bit, then -BANG- I was back in full, hot, glaring sunshine and the road ahead was steaming. Surprised by the number of vehicles on the road, I wondered where they'd come from.

Picking up speed blew the last rain off my visor and the flow down my back slowed to a trickle. The temperature was rising and without stopping the bike, I tried to unzip the sleeves of my jacket to let air flow up my arms. Distracted, I didn't see the next storm approach.

I spent the rest of the afternoon in and out of storms and the leathers kept the worst of it off me. Late afternoon sun peeked under the clouds and lit up a deluge of hailstones bouncing off the pavement ahead; the road was white with them.

"What do I do with this?"

Immediately they were cracking against my helmet and 'bonging' off the fuel tank. My hands stung from repeated hits despite the leather gloves. Cars were slowing down and some stopped. I kept moving, afraid to apply the brakes. The rain that followed was blinding and I was desperate for a bridge to hide under, but the storm ended quickly.

Dark skies still threatened and I'd had enough. At the Verona exit I got off and grabbed a secluded tent site. Several more wild storms blew through, testing the seams of the tent. The bike was under a tarp and every thing held up well.

Journal entry 1988: Riding in hail, a new experience on the first day, but it's one I'm in no hurry to repeat.

Tonight in the empty general store, I spoke with the campground manager. We talked quietly for a while about motorcycles, travel, and Gettysburg. Virginia gave up many sons to that battle and it's not forgotten here. The night was dark when I finally crossed the parking lot and faded into the woods by my tent.

3
MAMMOTH CAVE

I broke camp at 8 am wearing a dry T-shirt, wool sweater, and cold wet jeans. Damp leather went on before mounting. Slowly working my way out on the potted road, my enthusiasm was waning.

Gunning for Mammoth Caves in central Kentucky, I was still following southbound I-81, expecting to arrive there sometime mid-morning the next day.

Sore from yesterday, and struggling to find a groove, I began a routine of getting off the bike every ninety minutes and would keep it up all summer. By taking short frequent rest stops, I could usually push on all day.

The dawn ride was cold and tedious on this empty stretch. I'd expected to be enjoying myself more, and on past trips I would have been by now. Without a hard plan, the unlimited scope of the trip was overwhelming at first. Still, it was the prospect of more rain that was dragging at my spirits, and the hazy bright sun did little to cheer. Bad weather over the horizon would just have to be dealt with.

Two days into the trip and I was worried about finishing. I wasn't even clear what 'completion' would entail. Take one step at a time.

After a while, 'auto-pilot' took control of the bike as my mind roamed over a broad landscape. Traveling alone provided plenty of opportunity for reflection. Thoughts triggered by images, town names, even smells all competed for processing time, and this would continue all summer.

Un-commanded eye movement and an occasional sniff, recorded images in my otherwise empty helmet. Many of these images I can still recall clearly but can't put into any proper sequence. On two or three occasions I drove by something interesting without a care, only to turn around ten minutes later when it finally registered.

Just north of the Carolina state line, my route turned west, taking me down back roads toward Kentucky. I retain images of rough hills, with small towns and tightly winding roads. You wouldn't want to get lost in *these* woods.

At the end of the Civil war, the Army of Northern Virginia fled Richmond and made a dash for these western hills hoping to continue the war from here. They were stopped short at Appomattox Court House.

By midmorning, gas was my immediate concern. The bike got about sixty to the gallon, but with less than three gallons on board, had pretty poor range. Being Sunday, all of the few service stations I passed were closed.

Wet roads followed a wooded river valley through steep hills until I got to the town of Appalachia, where I filled up.

The next stretch of road, climbing the mountains to Cumberland, Kentucky was rough. For forty miles the turns were so tight and the grade so severe that the bike never got above third gear. Overcast skies and cool damp air smelled of rain, which was depressing. Long miles of switchbacks were grating, stuck as I was behind a small old car struggling to make the climb. The stubborn driver wouldn't pull over and let the long line of cars pass, and it was awhile before I could blow by and break free.

Crossing into Kentucky near the summit, the terrain was still rugged. Without thinking, I stopped quickly at a general store for a coke served up by a girl with no front teeth. While sitting outside the store drinking, the asshole in his little car drove past followed by the long procession of drivers who wanted to skin him (eventually including me, back at the tail end of the line).

Eastern Kentucky seemed a separate world - coal mining country and very poor. I passed one decrepit mining operation after another. All the big dump trucks were idle; evidently, operations shut down completely on Sunday. Not many people were out, giving the somber area the feel of being abandoned. Happy to have that stretch of road behind me, I started a long gliding decent down a backwoods valley, drifting out of the mountains.

By late afternoon, blinded by a glaring sun, I pulled onto the Daniel Boone Parkway near Cumberland. It felt good to move along at 70 again after all those hours at 35-40.

The countryside was hilly and beautiful. Sparse traffic clipped along, and "Mom and Pop" toll booths (which had the look of drive through general stores), were few and far between. There were thunderstorms about and the pavement was often wet. Fortunately, I missed the worst of the rain and my leathers were enough to keep the road spray off.

Over five hundred hard miles that day and I called it quits at the town of Columbia. I didn't actually see a town, just a strip mall and a cheap motel where I crashed. With the jacket thrown over a radiator, I showered then dropped onto the bed.

The bike had been running badly: no power and the exhaust sounds clogged. I'll worry about it tomorrow.

I woke to the smell of sun-baked pigeon and pulled my hot jacket off the radiator. Outside, the morning was cool with a deep blue sky. No wind - a good day for an early ride, with the sun just clearing the eastern hills. Sticking to the Cumberland Parkway there was little traffic and I drove slowly, enjoying the countryside. It was only an easy 120 miles to Mammoth Caves.

Away from the eastern mining operations, Kentucky was a panorama of well-kept farms and stables. At Glasgow I turned north-west to Cave City which was a collection of souvenir shops, a deli and a couple of gas stations.

The park campground was empty and I had my pick of sites.

Mammoth Caves is by far the largest surveyed cave site in the world. There are several hundred miles mapped to date with fifteen to thirty miles added every year. During the regular tours, the caves are lit by accent lights, many of them colored and tacky. Some of the larger caverns were impressive and defy description, but we couldn't linger in any area and were pushed along.

In the afternoon, I took the 'Lantern tour' and this was what I'd been hoping for. No lights except the flashlight you carried. It was the same sensation as night scuba. I tried to imagine how I'd find my way out with no light. The thought made my skin crawl.

There was a flash of an old memory - climbing down a rope to investigate the black void of an abandoned Nike Missile Silo. Flashlight beams from above reflected off the dark oily water to help guide me. The same curiosity that killed so many cats pushed me to go first (but it must have been just an old dream because nobody would ever be that fucking stupid).

Back at the still empty campsite, the early evening was spent checking out the bike and finding nothing wrong.

Journal Entry 1988: I made a fire, opened a beer, wrote the journal, and read. A distant rumble warned of coming storms. Ten minutes later the lightening was distinct, so I folded up the maps and kicked over the fire. Damp clothes drying on a line came down and campfire coals got doused. The bike was packed tight, everything in the saddles going into trash bags. There was a clearing fifty yards away where I watched the storms roll in. Before long, fat drops were smacking all around me. Breezes stiffened - then went to gale force. Cold blasts smelled of heavy rain coming fast. A blinding flash, a crash of thunder, and the sky opened.

4
ACROSS THE MISSISSIPPI

It rained hard all night and well into the next day. Sleeping in a dry tent with crazy weather is one of life's rare treats, but it has a dark side - breaking camp in a downpour sucks.

Journal Entry 1988: Rain was pounding against the nylon fly at 6 am. I keep putting off getting up, letting my few options play out for a while, but there was nothing more to do here. Even if I stayed another day, there was no guarantee that the storms would be past. If this weather system stalled, it could be raining for several more days.

The final decision was to keep moving west. Hoping for a break in the storm, I waited in vain. As much packing as possible was done in the cramped tent. As bags filled, they were carried into the rest room, followed by the tent five minutes later. The wet nylon was folded and stuffed into its bag, and then everything was loaded onto the bike.

I decided to just wear leather again and that was a mistake. In the ceaseless downpour, my clothes were soaked in twenty minutes, and the whole machine felt top heavy, unstable.

Leaving the park and taking back roads west, then northwest, the riding was slow. I passed through a series of small, deserted towns: Brownsville, Lindseyville, Sweeden, Bee Spring, each looking much the same as the others - wet, empty and dead. The droning engine was drowned out by rain pounding against my helmet, but the throb of the V-Twin was still with me.

In a dreary meadow, rain beat down on a cow chewing on the leaves of a low oak. She looked up as I passed by, but seemed indifferent to the dark weather.

Journal Entry 1988: Soft braking, wide turns, and thinking ahead helped keep the wheels on the pavement. I left my high beams on, and stayed several hundred yards behind the car in front. Twice I pulled over for impatient motorists behind. The day was grim, and 'Kentucky rain' kept pouring down.

After two hours of driving back roads, I reached the Western Kentucky Parkway and spotted a diner. I got no envious stares that day. Two men at the counter slid over and we talked about riding and, of course, the bad weather. One of them suggested getting onto the parkway and heading west until I broke free of the storm. He'd evidently seen a weather report, and it made sense. I'd be off course for a bit, but continuing north would have kept me in the rain.

An hour was wasted hiding in the diner waiting for the break in the rain that never came. Running out of patience after a quart of coffee, I took a long whiz then braved the storm: head west - keep moving. Ten minutes after getting onto the parkway the rain stopped and the sun came out. Dark thunderheads were around but the weather was clearly breaking. Soon there was more rain, then sun, and then rain again. I left the parkway and headed north.

Indiana was sunny and pleasant but I wasn't there long- only 36 miles across the south-west tip. Shirt off, I spent an hour sunning myself on a dry bank overlooking broad farmlands. Soaked to the skin, the sun felt good. My intention was to cross into Illinois on back roads, then make my way up to I-64 and on into St Louis.

Getting back on the bike I switched out of the full-face helmet. Don't know why, but it's hard to think in those things, and when there is a thought it seems to bang around inside and I can't shake it.

The Wabash River was slow and murky green; wooded on both sides it appeared timeless in the bright sun. A long narrow bridge popped up in the distance, then a deep rumble up a steep approach ramp onto the steel grate roadbed that I hated so much.

The Illinois tollbooth at the far end of the bridge

looked like it was built in the 1920's. With no cars in sight, a short stout man seemed to be dozing with his feet up on the desk.

I woke him, paid the toll then parked the bike to shoot some pictures. Now in his sixties, Chet had been collecting tolls here for a long time. We spoke for about ten minutes before being interrupted by a car heading east. A quick wave and I passed on.

Crossing Illinois was uneventful. There were still plenty of storms around but I managed to dodge them all. The hills had softened considerably and I thought about the prairies ahead. The bike was running well now and I had it flying, still heading toward St Louis.

Journal Entry 1988: For hours the compass needle was glued to "W". The ride was boring and my head emptied again as gusty winds blew me around like a tin can. I flashed by a modular home that was tossed off its trailer. At a service station, I prepared for rain again. The sky was dark all around and wet weather seemed inevitable. However, my luck held and the storms passed to both sides. An hour east of St Louis the skies finally cleared. The "Gateway Arch" appeared in the distance and I was surprised to feel a little thrill. The "Gateway to the West" is more than just a monument to those driving that way for the first time.

That 'little thrill' was all I was going to get. Cold, wet and disenchanted, it was stubbornness that kept me

going. There was nothing in St Louis that I wanted to see, but it was always understood that it would be the jumping off point. Good enough for Louis & Clark; it was good enough for me.

Crossing the Mississippi was a blur of traffic, but it was easy to be impressed by the river's size. On the west bank, not far from the bridge, there's a large parking area for the Gateway Arch with some old steamboats moored alongside. A side-wheeler converted to a restaurant provided a badly needed rest stop. The food was good, but I felt out of place. From the start, bad weather had impeded human interaction, and up until then that's all I thought it was. But in the restaurant, people avoided looking at me. The waiter took my order without making eye contact and I felt like an outsider looking in: a varmint, coyote.

As I drove up the steeply inclined parking lot, other steamboats churned upriver with pipe organs playing and flags snapping in the stiff breeze. It all seemed cold, artificial.

5
DOGGING THE OREGON TRAIL

Ignoring a quick impulse to go up into the arch, I left the city heading south west. Seven PM found me holed up at the 'Aces Motel', a rattrap on the outskirts of the city. My stuff was nasty wet and smelled. I needed to dry out under a roof.

Fresh out of 'Hotel Management School', Rob the owner, bought the place four days earlier for a song. I'm the sole customer and have the only room with a

Television. That TV had no connections but was wired to the office VCR. Rob's movie collection was limited to porn, which was already playing when I entered the room. I sat on the bed half watching, wondering how things had gotten to this point; certainly not how the trip had played out in my mind. Depressed, I turned the damn thing off, and started pulling wet clothes out of wet bags.

An hour was spent unpacking. Clothes were hung

on doors, knobs, over lamps - everywhere. Sleep was not in the cards, so I took a ride in the dark countryside west of the city, then gassed up for the morning. I made a few calls from a pay phone at a Mobil station before riding back. The room smelled like a wet dog when I got in and so did I. (This was the start of a growing road rat veneer that was hard to wash off.) I studied maps for an hour, then fell asleep on top of the bed in my sleeping bag, seriously doubting how much farther I'd get.

Dawn brought a beautiful day, but very cold. Moving along at 50 to 60 mph added wind chill to the mix. The sun would warm things up, but at 6 am, you just had to gut it out.

Ten minutes of gutting it out was enough for me, forcing a coffee stop. Still undecided about my heading, I poured over my maps at the restaurant. Should I head due west to Kansas City? or angle north-west along the Oregon Trail? Feeling better, I decided to follow the trail for a while and see where it would take me.

Journal Entry 1988: Passing St Louis was a milestone. Things felt different. Until now, the route was gloomy, scripted. The weather played a role, but it was more than that. There was a growing sense of being submerged and out of touch, with the full awareness that I was going deeper still. Black and white film was packed away, and I started shooting color.

Looking at the old images today I get the same impression as watching the colorized version of 'The Wizard of Oz' for the first time. The movie starts in Black and White, and then switches to color when Dorothy gets to Oz. I don't recall what triggered the change and at the time it seemed to be simply obliging a whim. I just never had the desire to change back.

For the time being I picked my way north-west across Missouri. The air was noticeably warmer when I left the restaurant and riding was more comfortable. The countryside was pretty, the roads were great for riding and the towns were pure "American Pie". The terrain was quickly transitioning to prairie and these low foothills were all that was left of the northern Ozarks.

My intention was to try and trace the Oregon Trail as closely as the modern roads permitted. I had several sets of US Maps. The big road atlas was packed, but I also used folding ones that would sit in a clear sleeve on top of my tank bag, showing the days route. The Oregon trail was clearly marked across it.

Over the course of the day, as I located places where the trail crossed the road, it became clear that I was wasting my time. Posts had been placed at these locations but all the signs had been stolen - a damn shame. There's not a trace of the trail itself; everything was completely overgrown.

I'd packed two cameras and a lens assortment. By late afternoon both of them appeared to be hosed. Pictures were a top priority and I couldn't be without a camera. After spending most of the day crossing the state on highway 36, I stopped in St. Joseph and bought another.

Historical Note: As navigation improved on the Missouri River, St Louis was abandoned as the Oregon trail's jumping off point in favor of river towns further west such as Independence, St Joseph and Council Bluffs. Thousands of migrants would swamp these towns in the spring, waiting for the season's grass to grow along the river bank trail.

Up until this point I'd always expected to drive across Kansas and Colorado, then veer into the South-West on the outbound leg. But even with glacier glasses, the late afternoon sun in this clear sky was scorching my eyes. To lose the glare, I headed north toward Rockport in the far corner of Missouri. On that whim, Kansas was scratched in favor of Nebraska as circumstance trumped reason.

The road north from St Joseph was snarled in rush hour traffic. I'd experienced this every day for fifteen years, but at that point it was alien; I didn't belong, had to get away. Another hour of hard driving and I set up at a rural campsite just off the county road. Less than five miles to the west was the Missouri River Bridge to Nebraska.

It was late afternoon, but there was still a lot to do. Boots and leathers were damp and needed time to dry in the sun. There were more night time chores than anticipated: setting up camp, checking and cleaning the bike, planning tomorrows route, cleaning cameras, unpacking and re-packing the bags. The bike needed to be repacked every night as the ratio of clean to filthy, bug crusted clothes changed.

All the clothes were washed that night so everything was clean and no problem to organize. "Laundry" consisted of stuffing every scrap of clothing into one wash load, then waiting for them to dry. For the first time I was faced with the dilemma of what to wear while the clothes were all being washed. The door was locked and I waited butt naked for the load to finish. Later I would pick up a pair of nylon shorts to wear while all the other clothes were washing.

Doing the laundry was an unexpected milestone: the completion of a full cycle of chores. Day to day activities now seemed more like a way of life. Later at the picnic table, I got the two older Minolta's working, so now I had 3 cameras. Things were looking up.

Journal Entry 1988: *After dinner I took a walk and watched the brilliant sun set across a meadow. There's a narrow band of trees to stroll through before reaching the pasture fence. Cows are grazing in the tall grass and gently lowing as calves nuzzle their moms. The smell of dew on the tall grass completed a bucolic vision of tranquility that seemed out of place in the 1980's.*

Tomorrow I'd cross into Nebraska, and it felt like the start of the main event. The wet overture had played itself out and the curtain was going up.

6
NEBRASKA

Journal Entry 1988: The morning air was clear and warm without a hint of rain. After breaking camp and driving up the gravel to the county road, I turned right and roared off - westbound.

It was only five miles to the Missouri River and Nebraska. The river seemed more than just a state line, it appeared to represent a cultural division as well. West of the Missouri, there was more brown than green, more pickups than cars, and more wind than I ever care to ride in again.

I started searching for traces of the Oregon trail, which intersected the road several times in the next hundred miles. The only indications were old markers along the road. Back in Missouri the trail was overgrown; here, any remaining traces through south-eastern Nebraska must have been plowed under a long time ago.

Journal Entry 1988: *The wind was from the south and had become uncomfortable. Gusts were hard and sharp and hit from the side. Each blast of wind moved me to the right, and I hogged the center stripe to keep as far from the ditch as possible. The gospel on landing a plane in wind wants you to keep up the speed, but that wasn't translating today for the bike.*

After a few hours I was beat. With the bike being moved around so easily, I hadn't been able to relax and enjoy the scenery. It was time to head north and get the wind behind me.

Changing direction helped. On impulse I gassed the bike and brought it up to 100. The ride was stable with no vibration. Noise from the draft drowned out the engine and the thrill was for real. Well on my way to 110, a woodchuck sat up on the roadside and looked at me. All I needed was to hit one of those. My brain switched on and I slowed to 60.

After an hour, all of my "North" miles were used up and I was forced to fight my way west again. At a rest stop a friendly trucker offered to let me ride close behind. I tucked the bike right in and it helped. Riding was easier but I had to stay alert - couldn't see a thing. The truck changed speed often and I had to occasionally hit the brakes hard. That was enough, and I decided to take my chances out in the wind where the road was visible. I beeped and waved a thanks to the driver as I buzzed by.

The road ahead was blocked by a big camper that had been blown over, and it took twenty minutes to work around it. People were injured, but there was enough help on the scene, so the throttle grip twisted and the bike rolled on.

Journal Entry 1988: By 7 pm the wind was starting to die down, making riding easier. The engine missed a beat and I was surprised to be out of gas. Reaching down I switched to 'reserve'. Two miles later while fueling, a pickup pulled alongside. An old man looked out and commented without smiling 'It'll be some time before you forget the Nebraska winds'.

This dry comment from a spectre of prickly old age, annoyed me. But that carping old fucker was right; I've never forgotten.

The rest of the day's ride was uneventful and the night was passed near Ogallala Nebraska, on the banks of the Platte River, along with the ghosts of hundreds of wagon trains.

Historical Note: The Oregon Trail now left the Platte River behind and followed the meandering North Platte. The trail was glued to river bottom lands that provided water, and grass for the livestock. After the North Platte, the trail followed the Sweet Water River all the way to the continental divide at South Pass

On the road again by 6 am it was a beautiful morning ride; Ogallala quickly becoming just a smudge in my mirrors. 'The South-West' was scratched for the time being. I was headed north-west, and for the moment, still following the Oregon Trail. That the sun was so hot on my back at this hour meant we were due for a scorcher.

For the first time I felt like I'd finally broken free. Until today there had always been wind or rain to contend with; but now, climbing up onto the high prairie, the odessey finally seemed to be in full swing.

Rolling dry hills obscured the horizon and there was no apparent agriculture. Endless brown lands were fenced, maybe for grazing - but I didn't see any livestock. Skittish antilope evaporated as the bike approached. They proved difficult to photograph and I gave it up after several attempts. (I was later able to get a few quick shots, invisible, with a bright sun at my back.)

Journal Entry 1988: Long stretches of the Oregon Trail are visible here, eroded ruts still denoting the route where wagon wheels cut into the sod. At points where the trail climbed or descended a hill, deep gullies, eroded by wind

and rain, mar the land.

Well over a hundred and fifty summers have fled, but the passage of almost half a million settlers has left deep scars that are slow to heal.

Journal Entry 1988: At long intervals I spotted distant cattle. A few small deserted parks along the way had exhibits, one featured a reconstructed winch built to lower wagons down a particularly steep hillside. It fires the imagination.
Back out on the empty road, the miles were endless.

Drifting over that empty land, one hill following the next, brought memories - sitting astride a surfboard bobbing in the swell. Back in '69', wave after long wave would roll beneath the board and all day long I'd choose among them. The head would empty, while memories, ideas and songs darted about.
Alone in that ocean of western Nebraska, it was the same. On some days I believe in God and on other days, science. That day following the North Platte, it was God.

Later there were quick stops at 'Chimney Rock' and again at 'Scott's Bluff.' Wagon trains slogging west, saw these as important landmarks on the trail, signifying the end of the great plains. For them, with the Rocky Mountains just visible on the far horizon, Wyoming was next. For me, it would be Dakota.

Geographical Note: Often described as 'flat', the Great Plains in truth form a long incline that gradually ascends from 450 ft above sea level at St Louis, to the 7411 ft. needed to cross the Continental Divide at South Pass. By the time the wagons reached Scotts Bluff, they had already climbed more than half that distance. At Independence Rock in Wyoming they'd ascended to 5739 ft. Crossing the Continental Divide was relatively easy compared to what lay further ahead – The Sierras.

Torn, I wanted to follow the trail further west to Fort Laramie and Independence Rock.

*"And sorry I could not travel both
And be one traveler, long I stood"*

Back in Ogalala I'd made campsite reservations in the Black Hills, and it was time to part ways. I normally never bothered to secure a campsite and could pitch a tent off road on federal land if need be, but this was the Memorial Day weekend and sites would be at a premium. Planning to set up a base camp for a few days, crawling into the woods on federal land wasn't what I had in mind.

Attempts to strike up conversations with people were awkward. They weren't much interested in talking to me; didn't like being reminded that I was there. Moving on, I cut the cord with the old trail and headed North.

Beyond Scott's Bluff, with heat rising in waves off the plains, the land was even more secluded. I was still in Nebraska following Highway 29, but only about twenty miles from Wyoming to the west. After a further hour of driving without seeing a soul, I crested a low hill and was waved to a stop by a lone construction flagman.

He told me a crew was paving the road ahead and I'd need to wait a few minutes. I turned off the engine and let it cool, put the bike on it's stand and popped my head out of the hot helmet.

"Where you headed" he asked.

"West" I replied vaguely

We spoke for a good ten minutes then I asked when I could drive on. "You can go anytime you want. I just thought you wanted to talk" he said.

"How do I find the fossil beds?"

"Straight ahead" he told me. Everything here seemed to be straight ahead.

"I know where there's a big turtle fossil, just off a dry creek bed out on the prairie" he said with a slow smile. Some night when I can find somebody to help me I'm gonna dig it out".

I toyed with the idea, almost rising to the bait, but in the end decided to ride on. It was still a long way to the Black Hills and I wanted to stop at the fossil beds. With a firm handshake I thanked him, then roared off the dirt shoulder in a cloud of dust.

The new road was like silk, and a mile later I zipped by the construction crew who didn't even lift their heads. Most of them were Native American.

I found the fossil beds after driving hard miles down a dirt road. The bike was difficult to control on the unsure gravel, and my feet were rarely on the pegs. Covered with dust, I parked then hiked a ways to a pair of distant hills. It was here that most of the fossils had been found. Many were still visible, but there was no sign of active excavation. On the far side of the hill near the top, I found a shallow cave where I sat for a good hour reflecting on my travels.

Journal Entry 1988: I expected to find open land in Missouri, Kansas and eastern Nebraska. Those areas are flat but they're definitely not empty. Not the kind of emptiness I see now. Here in the north west corner it's different. There's nothing to see but low barren hills, and nothing to hear but the wind. No people, no engines, no sound except the wind.

I was in Nebraska and heading north, not Kansas as originally intended. A few days earlier I'd turned North to get the sun out of my eyes, the easy choice – just following the path of least resistance. Sometimes my life had been defined by that strategy and I wondered if I let go of things too easily.

In two hours of driving and two hours of hiking, there hadn't been a soul in sight. Occasional birds flew by, catching the currents. Here the west wind had personality; it was a changing song of soft hisses and piercing shrieks as it built to a sudden howl. Alone, it was sinister, easy to hear voices on those airs – Zephyrus seeking me out.

My small cave had me out of the wind and the hot sun as well. I wanted to stay longer, listening to that enchanting wind, but it was time to move on.

Back on the bike, I slithered my way to the paved road. Then it was north through the Ogallala Grasslands, east for forty miles along US 20, before I turned north again just west of Chadron and on into the Dakotas.

7
DAKOTA

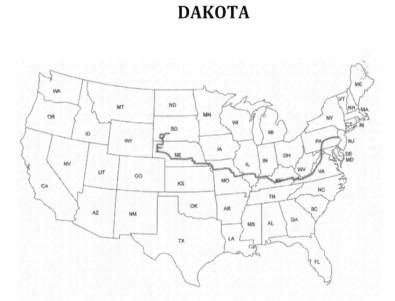

A big sky overlooked open meadows dotted with intermittent stands of pine. There was a lot to explore within a hundred miles, and it was time to settle in. A campground near Hot Springs, just south of the Black Hills, served as base camp. The small log cabin with bunks was stuffy, but still a welcome change from the tent. Just being able to cruise without the bulk of my bags, was worth the price of the ticket.

The day began at Custer State Park, which is not to be confused with the 'Little Bighorn Battlefield' in Montana. Most of the park consisted of long vistas filled with elk, bison, and mule deer. These park loops were hectic with cars, and for the first time, I felt crowded.

With all the visitor traffic, most wildlife had moved

far out away from the road, and I wanted to hike out. I'd been warned by a ranger not to get too close to the bison when taking pictures. "The calves are only a few weeks old and the cows are very aggressive."

I knew better. "You guys probably say the same thing about the T-Rex at Dinosaur National Monument". The ranger laughed, but I should have listened.

Another small clearing had mule deer, antelope, and wild ass. Bison grazed at a distance across an open plain. If they were truly aggressive, there was no safe approach.

Continuing on for a few miles I found what appeared to be an ideal opportunity to get a good shot of the herd. The road dipped into a gully before crossing a river on a long bridge. At the top, but back from the edge was a small grazing herd. Planning for only a couple of shots, I parked the bike in the hollow close to the bridge.

Laying the helmet on the rear seat, I metered and set up the camera lens in advance. The herd was upwind and wouldn't be able to smell me as I climbed to the top of the rise. It was a careful climb of about twenty feet and I was pleased with myself about the way I'd thought this through.

The instant my head cleared the top, there was eye contact with a cow who came for me in a heartbeat. I'm not altogether clear on the events that followed. Dropping the camera, I made it to the bike in four or five wild leaps, hearing her crashing down the slope behind me. Jumping onto the saddle, I remember the sound of my helmet bouncing off the pavement. I roared out onto the bridge, almost clearing the far side before stopping and looking over my shoulder. A six-foot head with horns was at the center of the span and closing fast.

With nothing more to leave bouncing on the pavement than my pride, I left the bridge behind, - flashing past a carload of Japanese tourists who were taking pictures of the incident and laughing at me (*assholes*). "She's your problem now Kemo-sabe!"

I waited for about 10 minutes before gingerly heading back to retrieve the camera and helmet. Half expecting to find bodies strewn across the bridge, I was surprised to see the area deserted. The Japanese had already retrieved their dead.

Historical Note: The Black Hills derive their name from the deep color of the Ponderosa pine that cover the slopes. The Lakota tribe has traditionally regarded the

49

Black Hills as sacred - an area of power. Surrounded as they are by barren prairie it's easy to understand why they were so treasured. The Black Hills were guaranteed to the Lakota by the 1868 Treaty of Fort Laramie. Then gold was discovered. A surveying party led by George Armstrong Custer travelled into the hills, documenting their finds, and revealing the natural wealth of the area. Word spread and prospectors filtered in, pushing the wildlife out and fueling a growing resentment with the native tribes, who were ultimately deprived of the land. In 1980 the Supreme Court ruled that the Black Hills were illegally taken and awarded the Sioux more than $100 million in damages; a settlement the Sioux still refuse to accept.

Journal Entry 1988: I drove through the Needles Area and climbed up to Sylvan Lake on my way to Mt Rushmore (where I'm sitting now writing this down). The "Needles" is an interesting ride through dramatic rock formations, weathered spires and short tunnels. The road is narrow and winds tightly through the crowded landscape.

At the top, Sylvan Lake was an area of stunning beauty. Crowded with picnickers and children splashing, this would have been better as a midweek stop, but I didn't begrudge their fun and moved on.

Geological Note: 'The needles' are spires of igneous rock that formed when magma forced its way up through soft sedimentary rock, then crystalized as it cooled under pressure.
Eventually the softer sedimentary rock eroded away as the hills rose, exposing the granite needles.

Rushmore was packed, but I'd expected it would be. It was something akin to a conveyor belt of 'ten minute tourists', coming to gape, check mark the box and then leave, quickly replaced by the next batch. I found a good vantage point to sit in the shade and escape the 96 degree afternoon heat. With my back against a stone wall I can see the faces: Washington, Jefferson, Teddy Roosevelt, and Lincoln. I've seen many pictures of this place and none have impressed me. My pictures

wouldn't be any better, but I'm glad I came here nonetheless – it's different in person.

There was a long conversation with an off-duty attendant about maintaining the monument. (Talking to anyone at this point was a treat). The sculptures take far more nursing than I would have guessed. I tried to

coax him into giving me a private tour up top, but that wasn't happening.

After a short talk with two bikers on their way in, I

took a wrong turn out of the parking lot and headed north. Catching the mistake a short time later on the compass, I made a long swing around to the west using back roads. Along the way, I passed by the Crazy Horse monument being sculpted from a cliff side. The site was just starting active construction and there was little to see.

A tour of Wind Cave National Park rounded out the day. Not nearly as impressive as Mammoth, I was bored and tired by the time we climbed out of the ground again. By seven pm, I was badly sunburned, and several beers to the wind, a mild depression had set in, fueled by a growing loneliness that would haunt me for the duration of the trip.

Up early next morning, I was headed east from Rapid City on I-90 - a brutally hot ride. Small wooden signs for 'Wall Drug' appeared on the shoulder, and they flashed by every quarter mile for the next hour. Each of those signs was unique and some were very clever, bringing to mind the old 'Burma Shave' signs of my childhood. The continued presence of these little signs was something I can't quite describe, but I paid attention, and looked for them. Suffice it to say they struck a chord, as many who have seen them will no doubt agree.

By ten, the thermometer was climbing into the mid nineties. In the far distance, a small dot appeared on the shimmering highway, but I couldn't make it out. Two miles later, I dodged a dead cow in the passing lane, bloated in the heat with all four legs pointing to the sky. The air was greasy with stink, and it took a while to shake it off. That's what Gettysburg must have smelled like in July of '63.

Fifty miles east of Rapid City, I pulled off at the exit for the Badlands. There wasn't much to see at the National Park Center - just enough to get a taste of the rugged country that stretched on for many miles. There were far too many people babbling to let me appreciate the setting.

Journal Entry 1988: The sun is beating down and the wind is blowing hard in my face. I'm alone, perched on a grassy ridge in an obscure area of the Dakota Badlands. Wanting to get away from the tourists, I followed a dirt road for miles. What I'm getting is more sunburn.

There's nothing but wasted land as far as the eye can see. Steep eroded bluffs smashed together in a tumble that defies description. This is the kind of terrain where you could become hopelessly lost in a matter of minutes. The colors are mostly varied browns but there are also some pastel shades of red and green. Not a hint of moisture. Signs on the road warn of buffalo in the area and I'm keeping a close watch. The sun is too hot to stay here any longer so I grab my gear and head for the bike.

I continued to ride southwest on the dirt road. However, the surface was getting soft and difficult to navigate. Keeping the bike upright required careful driving and constant concentration. I wanted to speed up and get some air on my face again but didn't press my luck.

Intending to drive for another 30 miles to "Wounded Knee", I gave it up. The air was too hot and the driving too uncertain. Not wanting to double back, I broke out the map for options. There was a road about ten miles off that headed north. This road turned out to be dirt also, but it looked firmer. In another ten miles

the surface was paved and I was out.

I'd planned to explore the sprawling Wall Drug complex on the return trip. But the parking lots were gagged with cars and passing up the chance, I headed west again. The bike was running smoothly at 80 mph, but the heat generated by the air-cooled engine forced me to wear leather chaps over jeans to protect my legs. The oil temp was right at the limit, and the hot running couldn't be doing the engine any good.

I stopped for dinner at a Pizza Hut just west of the campground and enjoyed talking to the family at the next table. Bob and Karen live in the area and were open and friendly. Bob was free with the advice but I didn't care. Pouring over folders of local attractions, I decided to pack out and push west again tomorrow morning. I wasn't sure of my route yet, but I was leaning toward Devil's Tower.

Driving back to camp, I passed 'Chautauqua Park.' The name was familiar but I couldn't quite place it. Late that night I remembered. Chautauqua's were nineteenth century assemblies that brought knowledge, entertainment, and art to rural communities. They are all but forgotten, fossilized as park names in clueless modern communities.

Devils Tower Wyoming

8
DEVILS TOWER

The overcast sky had just started to brighten when I packed out of the cabin and started north again. It wasn't the kind of dark, heavy sky that threatened immediate downpour; but sooner or later, it was going to rain. I faced three or four hours of driving and hoped the rain would hold off that long. The air was surprisingly cool after the heat of the previous days, forcing jacket, gloves and sweater.

My rear wheel was losing tread fast and I didn't want to ride wet roads with bald tires. Best I could figure was that long miles on blazing asphalt were the cause. The plan was to drive north into the Black Hills as far as the town of Custer, then head west on Rt. 16 toward Wyoming.

Just beyond Custer the road climbed up through

damp, dripping forests where small animals, startled by the bike, scampered into the woods. Mule deer looked my way with blank expressions and continued chewing.

A long, gliding descent through fragrant forests was my final impression of the Black Hills. Up ahead, northeastern Wyoming stretched out with its small gladed woodlands and open vistas. Herds of cattle were being worked in the distance, to what purpose I couldn't tell.

Pine covered slopes and broad valleys were sparkling in the morning light now peeping through the clouds. The air was sweet-scented with Balsam, reminding me of springtime hikes in the Catskill Region. As in the Dakotas, the woodlands had no undergrowth.

At Sundance, I headed north. The "Sundance Kid" picked up his nickname after he did jail time here for horse theft.

Historical Note: Devil's Tower was the first National Monument, designated by Teddy Roosevelt in 1906. Native American legend claims that a giant bear chased a group of maidens to the top of the tower, despite furious efforts he couldn't claw his way to the top. The long scars on the sides of the tower gave witness to the furious clawing. The true origins are no less dramatic. The tower is the cooled lava core of an extinct volcano whose sides have long since eroded.

Forty miles north of Sundance, at the top a high pass in the hills, I got a fine view of the next valley and Devils Tower. As large and monolithic in real life as it was on the silver screen, the tower completely dominated its surroundings.

Moving down into Tower Junction, I stopped for a

burger. Several other bikers were loitering outside. One of them had the most beat up leather jacket I'd ever seen. It wasn't even black anymore. I nodded but only got a casual look from them until they spotted the Jersey plates. Still worried about the condition of the rear tire, I asked about local dealers. There was one in Spearfish, two hours away in South Dakota. However, no way was I backtracking, the tire would have to wait. Ten minutes later, I was at the park office.

Campsites were available just south of the tower. After setting up camp, and scoping out the visitor's center, I set out on foot to circumnavigate the base. The trail was several miles long, with plenty of wandering into open meadows and gullies. Rock climbers were out in force. I sat for a while watching a soloist who was moving very slowly, carefully setting his protection, before moving on. I chatted with several women in a beginner's class who made their first real climb today. They didn't go to the top, but had a picnic about halfway up. It was easy to tell by their bright eyes and excited talking that they were proud of their accomplishment, and not a little glad it was over.

Excusing myself and wishing them luck, I continued around to the North side. Here the tower face was much smoother than on the south side where the sun's exposure caused a constant freeze/thaw in winter that fractured the surface deeply. There were scant visitors at the park, and even fewer of them out on the trails. The terrain to the north was almost park-like in its blend of pine forests, meadows and meandering streams. Yellow wildflowers lit up the ground in all directions, even in the drizzle. Only the grazing deer reminded you that this was all wilderness.

By late afternoon, I completed my hike and headed back to the tent. A light rain was starting to tap on the tent's fly just as I got the entry flap closed. In the distance, thunder was booming and the storm slowly grew in intensity. A flash of lightning, a crashing peal of thunder, followed by a lingering 'BOOOM' that rolled down the valley like a bowling ball.

I woke with a start. It was getting dark and the campground was quiet. Leaving the tent, I was surprised by how much colder the ozone laden air had become. For all the noise the storm made, it never rained much.

Starving, I drove the five miles back to Tower Junction to get food. The freckle faced woman at the general store, wanted to talk so I stayed awhile. For her there's nothing interesting about this place. She'd hung her loneliness up for all to see, but the words weren't really for me – I wasn't there. I'm just the next in a ceaseless parade of empty, anonymous tourists. Still, for both of us, it was half a notch better than talking to the walls.

Back at the campsite, sitting in the dark, I could see Devils Tower brooding; a dark mass against the night sky, it seemed closer than before. In the foreground, elk were grazing in the bright moonlit field.

There will always be things that can't be captured by the pen or the lens. Perhaps Ansel Adams could have done justice to the scene, but capturing that elusive air, in the moon shadow of the tower, was beyond my ability. Enchanted, I lingered at this window into a childhood dream.

The magic evaporated when a group of German climbers blew in and set up camp. They were loud and raucous well into the early hours, making it hard to sleep. It was the height of hypocrisy on my part, as I've kept many a campground awake in my time. Nevertheless, I'll fix their butts in the morning.

After a wild, but well orchestrated night of heavy storms, I'd be packing out for the Little Bighorn.

Soldier Memorial – Little Big Horn

9
THE LITTLE BIG HORN

5:30 am and the rain had stopped; but it was a cold 43 degrees on my little thermometer. I wanted to stay in the sack but knew enough to seize the chance and break camp before rain started up again. I let the engine warm for a good 15 minutes while packing out. There were groans from the other tents as the thumping engine drowned out the birds. I knew I was being an ass, but sometimes you need to pop a valve. "Sorry about that Kameraden - Auf Wiedersehen."

Wearing all of my remaining clean clothes, I was back on the road to Tower Junction by 6:30. My hands were frozen, even at the slow speeds forced upon me by the state of my tires.

A pickup driving across the prairie in the distance was kicking up a long plume of dust, which was incomprehensible with the roads so wet.

Heading due west, I rapidly left the last remnants of the Black Hills behind and headed out onto the Wyoming plains. Several hours of bone numbing driving got me to the town of Gillette where I stopped for food.

After so many days of traveling alone, I'd become isolated from the comings and goings of the world, literally on the outside looking in. There's not the slightest need or desire to know what day of the week it is. Difficult to describe, this sense of isolation was unlike anything I'd experienced. It's not loneliness and not necessarily unpleasant.

I usually came up for air in restaurants. Sitting in a real chair, reading a newspaper, I would at least get to talk to the waitress.

In cold weather like that, I'd draw out the stay far beyond just the meal, spread out the big maps and fine-tune the routes. Smaller maps were folded and sat on top of my tank bag in a clear holder. If the weather was bad, I'd inevitably get comments. And now the Jersey license plates were drawing attention as well.

A lifelong fascination with Custer's final battle ensured that the Little Bighorn was on the list. The only question was how to arrive. I'd wanted to head north to Busby, the final encampment before the battle. From there I'd pick up Rose Bud Creek and follow it to the Little Bighorn, just as the Seventh Cavalry did in 1876.

Rain seemed likely, and it was just too damn cold to make that plan very attractive. Once again, a compelling plan was discarded to follow the path of least resistance. There would be regrets later in the day that I didn't take advantage of the opportunity.

However, in a few days things were going to work out for me in spades. For most of my life, I've gone with the choice that felt 'right' at the time. Often it's been a snap decision and the merits weren't immediately obvious. There have been doubts about my resolve, and I wondered how others saw things.

When I left Lafayette College to join the National Guard, I hated every minute and second-guessed every scrap. In retrospect, it was one of the best choices I've ever made; I still reap the benefits.

If the path of least resistance feels like the right choice, it's not 'quitting' at all. It was time to stop being herded by metaphors; just do what I want and piss on the guilt. That kind of thinking won't fly with your mom, but everyone else can 'go fish' if they don't like it. In a few hours, I'd roam a Montana hillside littered with two hundred forty marble markers commemorating men who blindly 'stayed the course'.

A sketchy newspaper weather report reinforced a rumor I'd heard yesterday at the campground. There was snow ahead, a lot of snow. My vague plan had been to spend a night at the Custer Battlefield in Montana, then backtrack to Wyoming and head west to Yellowstone.

From the East, Yellowstone was reached via the East Gate or over the "Bear Tooth Pass". According to reports, both might be buried under many feet of powder with more snow coming.

"There's no room for snow in a primo motorcycle plan."

Best to just postpone the decision until I get to the battlefield, still several hours away.

With plenty of recent experience trying to dodge weather, it seemed certain that I'd need a place to hole up for a few days. I finished the last cup of coffee, akin to taking a deep breath of air before I drove back into the vacuum of the open road. There were many cold, empty-headed miles left to drive.

Across those barren plains, distant mountains, maybe the Grand Tetons, gradually rose up. The air was crystal clear and although still far away, they were very white and beautiful. However, the scene was also threatening; those peaks were set against a sky now filled with dark rearing storm clouds.

My heart went out to the pioneer families in their wagon trains who would have been faced by the same grim prospects. Hurried along by their determination to pass Independence Rock by July 4th, here it was June and the passes were snowbound.

At Buffalo I swung North toward Montana. The Bighorn Mountains, now on my near left, had some snow on their peaks, but not nearly so much as covered the mountains further off to the west. To my right were endless miles of bleak, scrubby ridges.

I could see the wind kicking up dust swirls or shaking the sage. Occasionally I passed a historical marker commemorating some half forgotten Indian Battle; I usually just read them quickly, and then moved on. One sign in particular grabbed my attention. "The Battle of the Rosebud – June 17, 1876".

Historical Note: The Battle of the Rosebud was fought between Crazy Horse's Native Americans, and General Crook's column of about 1000 soldiers. Crook's was the *southernmost of the three forces converging on the Little Bighorn. Crazy Horse's victory over Crook here at the Rosebud, helped set the stage for the rout, a week later, of George Custer's force approaching from the Northeast.*

Barren terrain where Crook's battle had been fought was all that greeted the eye. For me, it was something that helped bring to life the specifics of the Little Bighorn Campaign, but was otherwise meaningless. I spent a few minutes at the site then moved on.

There was nothing to distinguish the Montana border other than a lonely sheet metal "Welcome". This sign, like most others had been peppered with bullets from bored cowboys (or Indians). This "plinking" of signs from the passenger seat of a pickup, was a reminder that the spirit of the west was still alive, and that may not be good news.

The towns I passed were small and seemed relatively poor. This was Crow reservation, with towns such as Wyola, and Lodge Grass. These communities of small houses were exceptionally clean and well maintained.

About forty miles north of the state line I recognized the elevation that's been gradually growing

on the horizon. It's the infamous ridge that Custer's five companies followed in their attempt to outflank the confederated Indian village.

Journal Entry 1988: I'm confused by my familiarity with the ridgeline. I can't remember where I might have seen it from this angle. Perhaps there was a picture in National Geographic or one of the many other articles I constantly consume. I parked my bike at the Reno battlefield site just below the ridge. From here Reno's companies saw Custer waving from above - the final time those men were seen alive.

The Custer battlefield was a somber experience - one of the most fascinating stops. A melancholy mood seemed to seep from the ground. Unlike "Devil's Den" at Gettysburg, here the children visiting with their families were subdued. The landscape was covered with dry grass and low stunted bushes, much as it was in 1876. Looking around it's easy to picture the battle that erupted here; easy to picture the smoke and dust, the desperate faces of the troopers, and the final moments of swirling chaos.

The park service maintains the area where the last acts unfolded. It's roughly a square mile, from Calhoun Hill in the South, where the collapse began, to "Last Stand Hill", where tradition claims the fighting ended.

The summit and slopes of the ridge are covered with white marble markers. Most designate the spot where a soldier's body was found. Markers are scattered far and wide, but the bulk of them are clumped in four or five tight little groups; as remnants of companies regrouped, trying to hold off the avalanche.

"Last Stand Hill" has the Custer marker and about

forty others. A large stone monument also marks the soldier's mass grave declaring that they died while fighting "hostile Indians". This casual remark was understandably a bone of contention with the local tribes on the reservation in 88. I don't know if the inscription has been changed, although it seems to be an easy fix.

I spoke briefly with one of the park's Native American employee's. I asked her how she felt about the park's presentation of the battle. She said in a bored tone that in general they were comfortable with it. They would however like the park name changed and a native monument erected.

She was more articulate and expressive when going on about the Crazy Horse monument being carved in South Dakota. "Crazy Horse was deeply superstitious. He refused to let anyone take his picture. We can't believe that he would have wanted this monument".

It was my turn to suppress a yawn. I didn't know

for sure what she expected my reaction to be. 'Should we demand they stop carving the mountain? They're only trying to honor the man, and spending decades at it. Don't you have anything real to complain about?'

I kept my thoughts to myself, but she must have read my mind, and would have her cold revenge.

I asked a ranger about getting into Yellowstone. He made a call and found that all entrances except the North Gate were closed; but more snow was expected, and there were no guarantees that it would stay open.

Kurt Vonnegut might have written that the Custer annihilation occurred solely to provide me with a ranger for advice on the coming storm. When I continued on, that irony would rattle around in my helmet for the next forty miles.

The museum was filled with speculative pictures of the battle, mostly showing the old 'fatalistic' interpretation, as well as "stuff" recovered on the grounds. Several journals were found on the bodies of dead soldiers. One of them, a young doctor, had handwriting very similar to my own unique scrawl.

I felt closer to him than the others. What would a student of 'past-life' theosophy make of that?

If you have any interest in this bit of Custer history, take the time to do a little research. It's no longer the story you grew up hearing. By combining forensic archeology, and the all to often ignored Native American accounts, a clear understanding of what happened in the final hour is now possible.

A quick inspection of the rear tire showed no tread. There was one pay phone behind the museum, but I didn't have enough coins. By the time I returned with more, the phone was in use. The same woman with whom I had that conversation earlier, tied up the one phone for an hour and ten minutes knowing full well that I was waiting to use it. My thoughts will remain private.

Twenty minutes was spent in Deep Ravine, where the final fighting probably took place; as the last soldiers tried to scramble into whatever cover could be found.

Finally, the phone freed up and I found a dealer in Billings who stocked my tire. Billings was an hour of mindless driving to the northwest and the day was getting late. There'd be no camping at the Custer Battlefield.

I made it to Billings, pulling into the garage at six o'clock and got the tire changed by 7:30. The shop was ready to close and the job was rushed. They told me that they had no spoke weights and couldn't balance the wheel (Dude - What the fuck?). I had no choice but to pay up and hit the road, following the Yellowstone River westward another sixty miles to Big Timber.

Journal Entry 1988: The rear wheel was shaking badly and riding was uncomfortable. At about 9 pm, I pulled off the highway for a service stop. While filling the tank, I spoke briefly with a biker heading east on a Goldwing. He warned of snow up ahead in the pass near Bozeman. This wasn't good news, but my plans didn't have me going as far as Bozeman - turning south well before there, at Livingston. It may work out, but it might also mean that I could be driving myself into a corner. I grabbed a campsite and crashed.

Old Faithful - Yellowstone

10
THE GREAT VOLCANO

I came up for air in a coffee shop in Livingston Montana. With a table next to the front window overlooking main street, it was a good spot to watch the world spin by, people chasing after errands. My bike was in a shop a few blocks over. The rear wheel needed to be balanced and as long as it was up on the lift, I had it serviced, putting on new front rubber as well. There were still good miles left on that tire, but it needed to be changed sooner or later. With snow a possible hazard, I wanted deep tread on both wheels.

It had been a frozen start this morning, and I had my first fuel scare; the bike was well into "Reserve" when I got to town. I remember really sweating out those last few miles. Mileage had been steadily

worsening for the past two days. I guessed the problem to be altitude related, causing the engine to run rich. Combined with notoriously low octane for western fuels, the engine was working overtime.

When I picked up the bike, the mechanic advised me to remove the air filter, helping the engine to breathe more easily. (Re-jetting the carb would have been a better answer, but I couldn't be bothered.) I was traveling from 4000 ft. up to 7000 ft. that day so I took his advice.

There was a temptation to head straight west to the Pacific and warmer weather. Expecting it to be worn out and crowded, Yellowstone was never really on my high priority list of places to visit. Pictures of obese bears, milling crowds and overflowing garbage cans reinforced my tepid impression of the park. I was never enthusiastic about exploring here.

Way back in Missouri, my original thoughts were to head through Kansas and Colorado, working into the Southwest. However, a series of decisions prompted by stiff winds or glaring sun in my eyes, had conspired to keep me pushing north. Whatever the cause, I found myself following the Yellowstone River into the mountains ahead. Looking back now it seems like destiny, but at the time it just struck me as extremely unlikely.

Historical Note: Yellowstone was the first US National Park. Created by congress in 1872, it sits atop the active Yellowstone Super Volcano. The volcano's active status is attested by the scale of thermal activity:

geysers and hot springs, which are spread out across the park.

A cold drizzle was starting to fall as I followed the river south; the temperature hovered in the high thirties. On a good day, it was only an hour's ride to the park entrance, but I drove slowly, believing the road was about to freeze over. This would have been an enjoyable stretch of driving had I been more relaxed. The road ascended between the Gallatin Range to the West and the higher Absaroka Range to the East.

Journal Entry 1988: The Absaroka's were visibly buried under piles of new snow. Steam from unseen hot springs taunted me, before being whisked away on the breeze. Icy drizzle found a way through every crack in the jacket and I was getting cold. With the steady gain in altitude, the temperature couldn't have been very much above freezing.

The climb to the park was gradual, hardly noticeable. More apparent was the cold, which was starting to numb. The sky was getting darker and I hoped desperately that the rain didn't turn to snow until I could hole up.

Rain smacked against my helmet as I rumbled through downtown Gardner, where a lighted bank sign blinked out the temperature – '34 degrees'. Just south of town, the road made a hairpin left turn and I was suddenly at Yellowstone, confronting the massive black archway. There was a long moment of disbelief, as if I'd never really intended to be here.

I stopped the bike in the middle of the empty road. The place seemed abandoned, not a car in sight; the arch reared up like a tombstone. Here I was arriving out of the blue at the busiest park in the US, feeling like I was about to enter another reality. Engraved in the cold, wet stone was the dedication: "For the Benefit and Enjoyment of the People". But where were 'the people'?

Freezing, I stopped the bike at the gate window to pay. A young blonde ranger looked up through the

window, surprised to see an idiot on a motorcycle.

"You're a brave one," she said.

"More stupid than brave." I just wanted directions to the nearest dry corner.

Yellowstone contains several Villages dispersed throughout the park. The closest of these was Mammoth Hot Springs, about five miles in. It was still raining hard when I dismounted outside the lodging office. A large room held five or six very bored clerks waiting on non-existent customers. I approached one and asked for the closest room available. But shaking her head, she insisted that I wanted the "Old Faithful Inn".

"How Far is it?"

" A good hour south."

I shook my head back. "No thanks."

She patiently explained that people can wait years to get a room there; but the heavy snows had created a flood of cancellations. "In a few days the rooms will be gone." She insisted this was the chance of a lifetime and I reluctantly gave in.

The one-hour ride took three hours. The delay was self-inflicted, as I stopped at site after site.

I'd never seen so much wildlife, elk and mule deer, bison and glimpses of antelope. The slopes were covered with aspen and lodge-pole pine. I caught the sweet scent of Balsam.

The rain had stopped and the cloud cover was

breaking by the time I reached Old Faithful Village.

Unlike any building I'd ever seen, the inn dated from 1902 and was constructed entirely of undressed Lodge-Pole pine. Next to the front door a sign estimated when the next eruption of the Old Faithful Geyser would occur.

The lobby was an elaborate room at least five stories tall. Surrounding the lobby were three levels of balconies supported by pine trunks and branches. The handrails were all of branches as well. This is a place that must be experienced. After checking into my Spartan room and spreading my clothes out to dry on the heater, I tried to grab a quick nap. The room was so hot that I opened the windows wide.

Just barely asleep, a hissing roar from the open window had me leaping out of bed. It took a few seconds to get my bearings and a few seconds more to remember the sign next to the front door of the lobby.

At six o'clock, I took a short walk to scope out the immediate vicinity. There was plenty of wildlife and acres of hot springs to visit. These were particularly dramatic in the early evening when the steams and vapors were backlit by the setting sun.

In the end, I was most drawn to the Old Faithful Geyser. Even as a child, there were stories of Old Faithful. Expecting it would disappoint, I was startled by the howling intensity of sound just before and during the eruption.

You know it's comin' when it's comin'.

Addicted, I made a point of always knowing when the next eruption would take place.

Even when viewed from a rocker on the porch, it inspired, but when seen alone, up close in the predawn darkness, it could make your flesh crawl.

Journal Entry 1988: Back inside the lodge, flames were roaring in the stone fireplace, while a classical quartet, hunched over their instruments, played an unfamiliar piece. Guests were seated in chairs in front of the fire and all along the balconies - writing cards, chatting, or just sitting together soaking it all in. I felt a quick pang of loneliness before settling into a quiet corner on the second floor balcony.

At a small table, I brought the journal up to date, but struggled to find words to capture the range of today's experiences. After a while, I switched to the easier job of sending postcards. Giving up on plans for tomorrow, I moved to a rocker overlooking the lobby and let the strings fill my head. After dozing off several times in the chair, I called it quits.

The dawn sky was still overcast, but the air warmer. I was still unclear about the day's agenda, but with no clean clothes, I decided to do laundry.

Nineteenth century expeditions would stuff their dirty clothes into the geyser; letting the boiling waters of Old Faithful do the work. For me, the nearest Laundromat was at the park entrance in West Yellowstone, Idaho.

After dumping my clothes in the washer, I spoke briefly with a guy in a wheelchair. He claimed to have thumbed and wheeled his way south from Anchorage (the "BULLSHIT" light in my head was blinking). His legs were paralyzed and all his gear was folded up on the seat or strapped to the sides. Out of the blue, he asked me for a joint. I told him I didn't use the stuff, and he got irritated because I was "holding out on him" (The light in my head is now blinking "Narcotics Officer"). I told him to "Piss Off" and I meant it. Why are you targeting me? His seedy demeanor suddenly seemed 'sprayed on'. Clothes were dried, folded, and in the saddlebags. Then I got out of there.

For the first time at a base camp, I had nowhere special to be. Back in the park, green slopes crowded

with Aspen and conifers lined the road as the bike climbed effortlessly. The sun was out, with the sky a clear shade of blue that I'd never seen back east.

Overwhelmed, I had no idea where to begin, so I just got out and rode the north loop; putting in the effort to see as much as possible, while making time to absorb the reality of Yellowstone – a reality that was all around me. There was an undercurrent of doom, certainly not a premonition, just an appreciation of the raw power seeping up from the ground.

It was still early in the day but I was amazed at how empty the park was. I pulled into a dirt lot where a small group of people and a ranger were standing.

Journal Entry 1988: Across a broad meadow, elk cows were giving birth to this season's calves. They were at least two hundred yards away and difficult to see. Even with binoculars, it was left mostly to the imagination. If not for the ranger, none of us would be any wiser. Nevertheless we all felt privileged to be here."

I took the time to sit on the rim of the Grand Canyon of the Yellowstone. Colors were muted and this morning's cobalt blue sky was long gone. On the other hand, no people were around to spoil the sense of isolation.

Journal Entry 1988: Taken in the total context of Yellowstone, this is an amazing spot. There are no man made sounds to hear, just the rushing water far below. On the other end, away from my dangling feet, was an empty head - a pair of eyes gazing out from under a baseball cap. Large ravens were the only birds to be seen. One was sitting behind me in a dead tree. 'CRAK RAK RAK' she scolded in her sinister song. It's no stretch to hear voices in the animal cries. Elusive voices that just can't quite be made out. In the distance is a glimpse of Yellowstone falls,

a good next stop.

Moving eastward for eons, the Yellowstone caldera has left clear tracks on the landscape. Southern Idaho's "Craters of the Moon" still show those scars.

<u>Journal Entry 1988</u>: Almost every vista in Yellowstone includes steam rising, often dramatically. It's a constant reminder that this is the crater of an active super volcano.

Keeping that big picture in mind adds a degree of suspense. Someday this will all go up in a catastrophic blast."

At Lake Yellowstone, unique flora and fauna are found as hot waters from thermal streams, meet the cold water of the lake.

On the road back, I ran into several road construction projects. For miles I bumped my way over rough dirt roads, but it doesn't bother me any more.

<u>Journal Entry 1988</u>: Tonight the evening was clear for the first time in days. I spent considerable time casually walking the hot springs with steam rising against a backdrop of the setting sun. Deer and elk abound, with many chances to watch them at close quarters. Film consumption has been high and it needs to be rationed until I can find more. Before this trip, the sights I'm seeing now would have resulted in a photo frenzy, using up four or five rolls. Spoiled completely, I just relaxed and watched.

I hiked back to the lodge to see "Old Faithful" erupt again. I'm starting to notice that while the timing is pretty close, there's a lot of variation from burst to burst. The eruption is probably dependent on wind, and air temperature. In any case, tonight's was the best I've seen.

After dinner I met a college girl. I was sitting on the balcony listening to the music as usual, and she sat down next to me. I'm much more used to this type of familiarity among strangers now. She's probably lonely and wanted someone to talk to. Her name was Lily and she's here to wash tour buses. Before arriving at the park, she traveled with friends and we talked for a long time comparing notes. Lily highly recommended Glacier National Park. I've heard that recommendation before, but my plans will take me due south. There's been more than enough cold wet weather - It's time to warm up. Glacier will have to wait for the return trip.

The sun came up and I lay in bed for a while trying to decide what to do. I'd likely never return to many of these places. I also want to limit the amount of road duty per day. There are many weary miles between map destinations in the park, and far too many places to see. Maybe that's what the crow was telling me yesterday. 'You can't see it all. You can't see it all'.

"Well I can try to see most of it, even if I have to squish a few crows along the way. "

I'd been cruising slowly for about forty minutes when up ahead an elk cow crashed out of the bushes and crossed the road. A young calf was right behind her. Suddenly it froze in the middle of the road. The thing just stood there with all four gangly legs set apart looking wild eyed at me. It appeared to be bleating, but

I couldn't hear anything over the idle of the engine. Cars approached carefully from the other direction and stopped. Can this be one of the newborn calves? It seemed impossible it could be so big. Finally, the little guy spotted mom waiting patiently at the top of the

road embankment. He scampered up the slopes and

disappeared into the woods.

Most of the day was spent touring park roads with stops at Tower Falls, and Petrified Tree. I'd planned to drive the Bear Tooth Pass if it was open - it was closed.

Tower Falls, best seen from below, required a hike to the base of the canyon, still snow covered. With all the precipitation of the past few weeks, runoff was high and the falls thundered.

A good place to rest, I spent an hour here exploring, thinking and catching up my journal. Tomorrow I'd head south but still had no clear plan beyond the Grand Tetons. Climbing back up to the road, I said hello to a woman sitting on a rock eating an apple. She quickly looked away.

Returning to the inn early, there were chores to complete and I wanted to relax a bit. Sterilizing my contact lenses in a backpackers cook stove drew stares. Later I had a talk with a woman named Mary, who seemed to know the park very well. She suggested that I send my daily logs back to a newspaper at home. It would have been a good idea, but too late now."

Another woman started a conversation. She also worked at the park but had no wheels. She wanted me to drive her into West Yellowstone. A bit of a derelict, I wanted no part of her. I wondered briefly if she was a 'narc' like my wheelchair buddy, who also targeted me.

Journal Entry 1988: It's not lost on me how well things have worked out. The Inn is filling up as the snow is cleared and the gates are reopened. For the better part of a week, I was presented with an unheard of opportunity to enjoy this park in peace, on my own terms, without the chaos that comes with crowds. By my standards, this has been a blessing.

No one knew it yet, but this was the swan song for much of 'Old Yellowstone' - the end of an era. Storms that night were the last Yellowstone would see for many long months. It would be the driest summer on record, and in a few weeks, lightning strikes created the first fires. Stoked by high winds, abundant fuel, and no rain, the firestorms began. They were quickly out of control, and all efforts were focused on saving the villages. Much of the wildlife would perish, almost certainly the newborn calves. About 800,000 acres were impacted, and for the first time in history, Yellowstone was closed to the public.

A supreme effort would save the Old Faithfull Inn, but fires destroyed over a third of the park. It would grow back for sure, but not in my lifetime.

11
SOUTHBOUND

Journal Entry 1988: *Grabbing a quick breakfast, I was out the door of the Inn by 9. The bike was packed and loaded in five minutes. The repeated drill of loading is well polished at this point. In the back, the duffle straddles the*

passenger saddle right behind me, supporting my shoulders and permitting me to lean back as I ride. It was a beautiful morning, cold but clear and very likely to get much warmer as I descend to lower altitudes. Heading south, I had to stop and put on more clothes. I passed Lake Yellowstone to the east. There's almost no traffic on the roads, which is surprising as it's not very early."

*As I passed beyond the boundaries of the park, I had the distinct feeling of leaving a sanctuary. Sitting atop its ticking time bomb, the park is a magical 'Shangri La' where the rest of the world is locked out. That I've never seen anything like it, goes without saying. There **is** nothing else like Yellowstone.*

My enchantment evaporated as the miles zipped away beneath my mud-splattered boots. I felt like I was back in a mundane world of deadlines and obligations. There was a feeling of depression; a sense that the vacation was over, although the weeks still stretched ahead, well beyond my minds eye.

Grand Teton National Park is about 80 miles south of Yellowstone. I don't know very much about the geology of the area except that they are considered the youngest of the Rocky Mountain ranges. They looked very different from other ranges, primarily because, from the east, there are no foothills to obscure the view. Sharp, jagged, snow covered peaks, stood out in bold relief, looking much like a photographic backdrop. On the eastern side, broad meadows filled with yellow flowers stretched right to the foot of the mountains. A clear lake appeared that reflected a complete alpine vista. The beauty was breathtaking, even though I suspected the photos would disappoint me.

Little time was spent here. There was an interesting Native American museum, and I spoke to a ranger about what the park had to offer. Most of the

best features were backcountry experiences, and I wasn't equipped, nor did I have time to spare hiking in alone. I moved on.

About a hundred yards in front of me a bull moose was standing in the middle of the road. I pulled in the clutch, thumbed off the engine switch, and rolled to a stop on the side of the road. Very carefully, I eased the camera out of my tank bag. I checked my settings quickly as I expected to get only one shot. (The clamor of an SLR mirror slamming often spooks wildlife.)

Suddenly a carload of tourists came backing down the road at high speed, and the moose bolted. I'd read an article claiming that 12% to 20% of the world's male population is descended from Genghis Khan. Hard to prove but it would go a long way toward explaining why there are so many assholes.

Jackson Hole Wyoming was a big ski town in the winter, but there wasn't much going on then. I could see the ski slopes all around, mostly green, with snow

only at the peaks. Nothing caught my eye as I cruised through town. I didn't really give the place a chance, but so what? Following route 191 south into Utah was now the plan for that day.

Journal Entry 1988: Post Yellowstone depression was setting in, and I'm in a dark funk. For several hours the road winds through tree covered hills, jumps narrow gullies filled with crashing streams, then glides down into a broad green valley. With the Wind River Range to the east and the Wyoming Range on my right, the road ran straight as an arrow just west of the continental divide.

After about forty miles, the terrain quickly transitioned to bone dry prairie. It's hot and I took the opportunity to shed clothes, tucking them under bungee chords. Spotting a small group of antelope standing on a knoll, I was able to snatch one quick shot before they skittered off.

The road is lined with wire fencing on wooden posts that stretch off to the horizon. Every forty or fifty miles, a small town appeared as a wavering dot in the distant haze. These towns were faceless and dreary. They all looked the same: a bar, gas station, café and always a dance hall. I would slow to thirty, roll through the empty town, then watch them gradually fade away forever in the rearview mirrors. These towns seem to drift back to a late nineteenth century America that maybe they never left.

Lifting my hand, I waved at cowboys working a herd. They nodded but didn't wave back. It sure looked like a tough way to make a living. There was a marker on the road and I guessed it was for the Oregon Trail. A quick turnaround, and sure enough, it was my old companion; there were few other clues to its existence, just a dirt road - two ruts heading west toward a vanishing point on the horizon.

Historical Note: This was the "Sublette Cutoff", a shortcut saving fifty miles for anyone not needing to follow the main trail south to Ft. Bridger.

Part of me wanted to follow. About twenty miles to the east was "The Parting Of The Ways" where the Sublette Cutoff and California Trail separated. Driving there seemed like a waste of time that day, but I'm glad I did. In a few miles, I must have crossed the main Oregon/California trail that passed through Farson, but there was no indication that I could see.

The road rolled by long stretches of range grass and wire fence. At a gas station I took the time to grab a beer and watch the Lakers take a drubbing from the Pistons. The station owner was an LA fan, so I rubbed it in a bit. He was a good guy and I regret not jotting down his name.

Later, at Rock Springs in Southern Wyoming the temperature topped 98. I pulled into a fast food restaurant just south of I-80."

Chewing mindlessly, I stared at passing trucks with red eyes. This had been an endless, grueling day. A far cry from the mystical experience that other writers claim, the bone numbing reality of motorcycle touring is exhaustion, dehydration, disorientation. My vacant eyes seemed to be nothing more than rubber stoppers that kept my liquefied brains from spilling out over my face."

The map lead me West on I-80 for about five miles before heading south on 191 again into Utah. Hills were becoming more pronounced now and greener.

Driving far too fast down that badly washed out road, I showed not a flicker of interest in Flaming Gorge National Recreation area, just to the west. At about 4:30 I crossed the Dam and stopped briefly on the far side to catch my breath. Arms were burned to a crisp, as was the lower part of my face below the sunglasses. After chatting briefly with other tourists, the leather jacket went back on to protect my arms despite the heat.

Thirty five miles further south I took a tent site near Vernal, twenty miles west of the next stop, Dinosaur National Monument."

After a Pizza Hut dinner, I took out the wrenches and checked over the bike. Everything was ok, but I put the air filter back on, and that should have happened a long time ago. Not so high up anymore and there's a lot of dust blowing around. There wasn't a tree to speak of in this campsite, just dry grass and dry wind.

Journal Entry 1988: The early evening sun is bright red and except for the wind slapping tents around, this area is quiet. Other campers are talking in subdued tones. The scene has a timeless quality, but I can't explain why. Maybe it's how I'd envision an Oregon Trail wagon campsite. Everybody too exhausted to do more than whisper - anticipating the day ahead, while trying to forget the ones behind.

12
DINOSAUR TO ARCHES

Journal Entry 1988: _An early start today, but even at 7 am, there's not a breath of fresh air; it's going to be hot. Taking Route 40 east, I passed through Naples, then on to the main park entrance at Jensen._ _Hardly towns at all, there's nothing about them to encourage a memory. Turning left onto a side road I headed north into the park. The road quickly turned to dirt, but it was flat, firm and very drivable._ _After a few miles, the road completed a half circle and I seemed to be driving south again into a parking lot and the dinosaur quarry._ _I spent a couple of hours in_

the park building (as much because it's air conditioned as for any other reason). Constructed of glass, the building enclosed an almost vertical slab of rock containing hundreds (or thousands) of fossils. Formerly a mud bar in a river which collected carcasses, the bones fossilized, and then the whole area was pitched upward to its current angle. On the face of the rock were several technicians dressed in white that were continuing the job of exposing more fossils. The work appeared to be mind numbing.

Dinosaur is one of the larger National monuments. In spite of its size, there wasn't very much easily accessible. I left the Dinosaur Quarry and headed further east. Another dirt road took me backcountry into an area with marked hiking trails. The land was barren and very dry. I hiked through several isolated canyons where native petroglyphs were still visible; painted, or sometimes chipped into the rocks. The sketches appeared to be drawn with pastel colored natural chalks. Pictures included humans, animals, and even doodles. Very faded with age, they're further damaged by bullet holes, where some jackass relieved his boredom. I have no way to know for sure but they all appear to be drawn by the same hand.

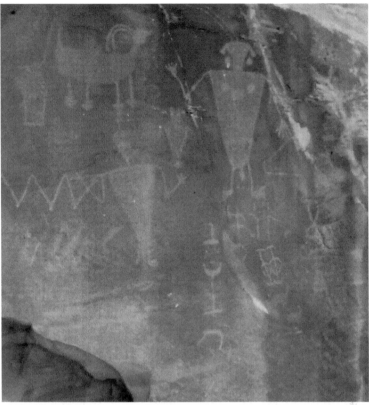

Journal Entry 1988: Even now in the 20th century, this is an incredibly remote area, and this little corner seems to have been a very private place for someone, perhaps a shaman, or a series of shamans

No one else was out in the canyons; visitors seemed to hit the main attraction for an hour then would roll on. They missed the best stuff. I took advantage of the visitor center one last time to cool down, before driving south.

Once again, I had a choice. To the southeast was the Black Canyon of the Gunnison and to the southwest, Arches National Park. I didn't need to decide for at least ninety miles but then I'd have to choose. I gassed the bike at Dinosaur, Colorado, another one pump town, and then headed south on Rt. 139 running down the backside of the Rockies. The land was dry with low hills

and scrub brush. There were no towns and I don't

recall any buildings and few intersections.

The roads were good, but the going was slow; this was 'open range'. I'd driven 'open range' before without understanding its implications. In brief, it meant that cattle run free. On this stretch cows were everywhere, and on two occasions the herd was blocking the road. I had to ease my way through these groups, more than a little tense. Some of the animals startled then bolted; others appeared curious and were reluctant to move - very nerve racking. There were short stretches where the range was closed, between ranches I guess.

The animals were kept from wandering down the road by grates installed in the surface of the asphalt. Cows wouldn't cross the grates. Further south I saw grate simulations that were merely painted on the road. Obviously, the effectiveness came from the visual pattern created.

The choice was made – Arches as much because I didn't want to drive further east than for any other reason.

After gassing at Dinosaur, I'd not seen a pump. This was the last place I wanted to run dry. At Loma, I saw several stations but they were closed because it was Sunday. I switched into reserve and headed west on I-70. Running down the hill on what must have been the last half pint, I rolled into Crescent Junction, Utah and filled.

Arches National Park is located thirty miles south of Crescent Junction on Rt. 191. I learned at the park office that the campground was full, and there wouldn't be any openings for the next few days. I hadn't counted on this, as every other park had plenty of openings. The campground was located twenty miles into the park, right where the pavement ended. I decided to drive it and see for myself.

As the sun slipped lower, massive rock formations cast enormous shadows and the boulders were alive with color in the afternoon sun. The air was dry and clear. In the distance, the purple La Salle Mountains stood out on the eastern horizon. These were amazing vistas, whose colors deepened as the afternoon progressed. Rock formations and arches grew more dramatic as the sun started down.

It was immediately obvious why the campground was full. There aren't many sites and they're unusually attractive and private. Set among huge boulders, each site was isolated from the others; the views were great, there was plenty of adjacent hiking - but no room for me.

It was a slow, reluctant, ride out, stopping for a couple of short hikes on marked trails. The ride back was equally dramatic with the sun setting. This would be a beautiful place to linger but I had to find a campsite. In Utah, you can camp almost anywhere, but I needed a shower badly and was in no mood to sleep on the side of the road. Luckily in Moab, I got one of the last campsites. Nothing to brag about, but it had a shower and a pool. After making camp and cleaning off, I drove back into town. It was jumping. Dinner and a beer at a hole in the wall Italian restaurant raised my spirits for a while; unfortunately, the waitress was harassed and didn't want to talk. I paid the bill and left, alone in a crowd.

The pool at the campground was roaring with excited kids having a blast. Bobbing in the corner, minding his own business was an alien, just recently sneaking in from the wild. All of what he could see made sense, it was nothing new, but it wasn't where he needed to be right then. However the world wasn't just about him and what he wants, there was a broader context and he knew it. He had a choice, get out of the cool water or deal with it. He stays.

Journal Entry 1988: Refreshed by the pool, I went for the tent. On these hot still nights, the tent's rain fly stayed off, increasing airflow. However, despite being cool, clean, and comfortable, sleep won't come - too tired maybe. Today has been one of the toughest grinds. Reading doesn't help because my brain won't stay put. The hardest piece of the trip was coping with the loneliness. Out on the open road or in isolated parks I hardly notice, but when entering an area with lots of people, particularly resort areas with families and couples, I feel like an outcast traveling in a bubble, invisible to the world at large. Everyone knows everyone else, except for me.

Sometime after midnight, a sharp wind pounced upon us, like an Eagle grabbing a mouse. A series of hard gusts of 40 – 50 mph struck the campground. I heard curses and shouts as tents blew over, and a wild scramble to get them up again started. It occurred to me now that each of these families was alone as well. They had each other, but didn't know anyone else. I dressed and helped a woman traveling with kids set her tent right again. I wasn't the only one getting up and pitching in. There was sleepy laughter, handshakes and 'thank yous'. It felt good.

Eventually the campsite quieted down again, although the restless spirit of the wind would badger me for several more days.

13
THE CLIFF DWELLERS

There was only the faintest suggestion of dawn while packing out. Breaking camp was annoying in the persistent wind and blowing dust, but it presented no real problems. Continuing south on 191 there was no stopping for breakfast; I was rushing to my next destination - Mesa Verde, the new base camp.

After being shut out at Arches, I wanted to be sure of a site where I could spend a few days. The wind was coming from the south, directly in my face and not a problem. The ride was typical Utah scenery, dry brown bluffs and intricate rock formations. I passed Wilson Arch on my left but didn't stop. It was a large well shaped feature, but being next to the road and unprotected it had been trashed with graffiti and litter.

Tanking up at Monticello, I headed east onto Rt. 666

toward Colorado. Now the wind, hitting me broadside, was a real problem. Gradually the needle on my handlebar compass swung to the southeast and the gusts became less of an issue. At the state line, the governor of Colorado reminded me to "Be safe and wear my seat belt" – thanks man.

The sun was up and full in my face. Driving directly into the glare was uncomfortable, even with the glacier glasses. Sunlight in this clear air was so intense that I was forced to look down and rely on the short stub of a rim that I'd snapped onto the helmet.

It wasn't safe driving this way, particularly since I

haven't slowed. After a bit, I caught up with a lumbering RV and tucked in behind. That did little to block the sun but it helped me stay on the road. I could watch it in my peripheral vision as I keep my eyes down.

By midmorning I'd reached Cortez and turned due east on Rt. 160. Another ten miles got me to the park entrance where I found the campgrounds empty. I took some time choosing between unremarkable sites. There was nothing special about any of them, dry and un-shaded, but adjacent to natural areas and hiking trails.

The tent became too hot to rest in until I clipped a foil survival blanket over the top and the reflecting side shed much of the heat. I can well remember the smell of hot 'ripstop' nylon.

By noon it was time to explore the park and I headed toward the mesa proper forty minutes to the south. The road climbed through hills and snaked along gullies. At one point I passed through a long unlighted tunnel filled with busses and campers.

With no places to pass, we moved at the speed of the slowest RV. Impatient drivers behind me rode right up on my tail to my considerable irritation. I pulled off the road and waved them by with a hand gesture that I hope expressed my contempt. Tailgating is a hot button, but I've learned that on a bike the only real option is to get out of the way and try not to get angry. I failed that test.

The park was far more crowded than I anticipated. Tour busses were everywhere. Most of the tours were European, particularly German. Where are the Yanks? Expansive parking lots were packed solid, but I wasn't concerned. This was just a test cruise to sample the highlights. I'd be back late in the afternoon when I thought the park would be quieting down.

Journal Entry 1988: I was struck by the large number of ruins in the area, not only in among the cliffs but atop the mesa as well. Most people are familiar with the 'Cliff Palace', but I'd always imagined it existed in relative isolation. There appeared to be dozens of cliff dwellings in the immediate area, which must have supported a large population. The ruins on top of the mesa were not as popular (or crowded) so I stopped the bike and explored the old villages in detail. Evidently, these buildings predate the cliff dwellings by many years. It's unclear what pressures moved the population down from the mesa into the cliffs. It could not have been more convenient. There's also only speculation as to why the tribes abandoned the region entirely a few centuries later. My guess was that they found something better. This is a great place to stop and explore, but I wouldn't want to live here.

Historical Note: *Modern archeology has suggested that extended periods of drought and unusually cold weather, forced the abandonment of the mesa villages.*

I headed back to the campsite to eat, stopping at the store to grab food and a coke.

Putting down the journal after an hour of fruitless effort, I explored one of the trails leading west out of the campground. It was well marked and scenic, with plenty of dramatic rock formations. On the return trip, a small group of deer caught my attention on the trail. The sun was low on the horizon coming over my shoulder. The deer turned to look repeatedly, but couldn't make me out in the glare, even though I saw them clearly. It was an odd sensation, stalking something that's in plain sight. Closing the gap carefully allowed me to get about fifty feet away before they bolted.

Later I took the time to peel off a label that's

attached to the bottom of my windscreen. It warns me in no uncertain terms that this windshield will not protect me in the event of an accident. This thing had been annoying me for 6,000 miles and I've had enough. Next, I cleaned the bugs out of the whistles. They were packed in solid, and it took 25 minutes of focused work to get them clean with the toothpick on my pocket knife (that I'll never again put in my mouth).

By early evening, I'd returned to the cliffs along the mesa. It was wise to wait. The crowds were gone; the air was much cooler, and the late afternoon shadows added a nice dimension. It was no cakewalk to climb down to the cliff palace. I wondered again what would motivate the tribes to move down from the relative convenience of the upper mesa. Concentrating on photography, I took a series of carefully composed pictures, but it was hard to get clean shots with so many tourists. A good bit of time was spent sitting and watching from various vantage points. There was so much to absorb.

I chatted briefly with the ranger but she was watching the clock, counting down to quitting time. In a few more minutes, we were herded up the ladders to the parking lot. The ranger drove off, so I climbed back down, took a series of shots with no people cluttering the scene, then sat on the ledge overlooking the canyon.

An evocative setting, I was struck by the way noise carried; could hear conversations from a great distance and although muted, some of the words were distinct. I tried to imagine the variety of sounds that must have echoed on a hot summer night when the cliffs were populated. Muffled adult conversations, barking dogs, and the squeals of playing children would have filled the air. The wind added notes of its own. I glanced across to the parking lot atop the far mesa where a ranger was 'big waving' me to get moving.   I waved back and climbed up to the bike.

It was a long ride to the campground and there was no rush to get back. Mesa Verde was off the beaten path and it was obvious that I'd never invest the time to come here again. These final lingering hours roaming the park would have to hold me.

Late that night I took a walk to one of the small meadows about 400 yards from my tent. The glade was surrounded by low trees and lit by the soft glow of an almost full moon.

Looking forward to something completely different, tomorrow's plan was to drive out of the park to Durango and take an excursion on the old steam railroad there. Completely relaxed, I drifted off half asleep, though my eyes were still open. Like phantoms, two deer walked into the clearing no more than twenty feet away. They started to graze but one of them, a buck, lifted his head and looked directly at me. Our eyes met and there was a momentary connection, then he resumed grazing. I'm well aware that the deer are acclimated to humans here at the park, and this was no magic, still the moment was real just the same. Eventually the deer moved off and the spell passed. Like awakening from a pleasant dream, I tried to hold on, but it was too late. Returning to the tent, I dropped into a leaden sleep.

It was late morning when I woke, and I stayed in my bag for a good bit longer. Weeks of relentless travel had worn me down, even though my stubbornness wouldn't acknowledge it. By the time I got to Durango the last of the rail excursions had left. I tooled around the shops in town for a while, buying gifts and grabbing lunch. I also took the time to get the bike serviced at a shop just outside of town. It was a scrawny teenager who was manning the store and he appeared to have the attention span of a potato chip. I watched him like a hawk but he did a thorough job.

The ride back to Mesa Verde was about thirty miles and I spent it thinking through tomorrow's route. In all probability I'd move on to the Grand Canyon. A brief moment was spent toying with the idea of visiting the Chaco Canyon site in New Mexico; but I'd had my fill of ruins for this week, and the thought of eating dust on long stretches of hot dirt roads killed that plan. Tomorrow would be a busy day with stops at Four Corners, Monument Valley, and Painted Desert before I got to the GC.

The high tide of tourist busses was receding when I

came back in. I washed clothes, and then late in the afternoon drove up onto the mesa for a last look.

Avoiding the cliff houses, I returned to the villages

up top. One that I'd not explored before was large and empty. I walked in a few hundred yards well to the back and found a kiva in a group of houses. It was a good place to sit and contemplate. How many others, for hundreds of years, had sat at this same spot, with each generation passing the torch on to the next.

I took my time and just meandered among the ruins. This has been a good base.

Historical Note: Kivas at Mesa Verde were round rooms generally used for ceremonial, religious and sometimes domestic purposes.

14
CHINDI - BAD SPIRITS

The air was cold and the sky hazy that morning. I broke camp at around 6 am, gassed up at Cortez, and then headed southwest toward the 'Four Corners' Area. The scenery was nondescript."

Four Corners is the only location in the United States where four states come together (Colorado, Utah, Arizona, New Mexico). I'd planned to stop there from

the beginning, but now wasn't very enthused. There was nothing to distinguish this spot from the hundreds of square miles of barren desert surrounding it - just an accident, a political curiosity that's not worth dismounting to see. Other people go out of their way to see this place, but I drove by without a glance or a second thought.

My visit to New Mexico lasted less than a minute. Route 160 snips off about a half-mile of the north west corner of the state. Hardly a visit but evidently the residents took it seriously. There was a big 'Welcome to New Mexico' sign on the road, and a half-mile off in the distance is the 'Hasta La Vista' sign. There isn't another road I could turn onto if I wanted to stay. 'Hasta La Vista?' Are they Sane? The oddness of this scene bounced around inside my helmet. Can't quite get my hands around why this doesn't rub right.

Just after passing Red Mesa, I headed north on Rt. 191, riding back into Utah for the third time. A bit of a detour for sure, but necessary if I wanted to see Monument Valley.

This was Navaho Reservation and it seemed an unhappy place. For the first time I was extremely uncomfortable traveling alone. Earlier, right after heading west on Rt. 163, I'd passed an old pickup truck with no muffler, and a pack of kids in the back. I waved to them as I passed and they gave me the finger - 'Ok I get it'. The truck picked up speed and a mile or so later I heard him creeping up on my rear fender. I'm doing 60-65 and didn't want to get into a race, so I pulled ahead then turned onto a side road - a big mistake. He followed, and I was cornered. A quarter mile down the road the pavement ended and the surface turned to dirt. I was in trouble. Driving recklessly fast, with the pickup in hot pursuit, his engine roared over the sound of mine. It's hard to say whether this was just intimidation, or a serious threat. Either way I could drop the bike and go down. Very scared, I made a right turn onto another dirt road, which wound through rough terrain. After a few miles, I saw pavement again, then a hard leaning left back onto 163, hardly slowing for the stop sign. The pickup also blew through, but this game was over. A quick down shift and my right hand had the throttle to the stops. The bike responded, rocketing well past 110.

I started to lift my middle finger, but reconsidered, not wanting to give them an excuse to keep after me. Quickly the pickup became a dot in the rearview, then nothing.

The few miles to Mexican Hat were nerve wracking, and I'd been badly spooked, but once on pavement again I was better, in much better shape than after the 'Buffalo Incident'. At least Japanese tourists weren't standing roadside to mock me.

At this speed I knew I needed to stay alert; but gradually, my attention drifted as the helmet slowly regained control of my head. I wondered about the origin of the name "Mexican Hat". As if in reply, a sign announced 'Mexican Hat Rock – 100 Yds'. I looked to the left and got a snapshot impression of a large Obelisk with the top part shaped like an inverted Sombrero - so much for names.

I came into town far too quickly, braked hard, and got my first look at 'Mexican Hat'. I hid out behind a service station until the pickup drove in. Five minutes later, the truck moved back out the east side of town, ending my debate as to which direction to take.

Monument Valley struck me as similar to Arches National Park but not as beautiful. There was a lot of trash, the towns were dirtier than they needed to be, and turquoise jewelry stands squatted in each photogenic locale. I didn't dare head down a dirt road for a better view. Still early in the day, the sun rose over my left shoulder. The morning haze had vanished without my noticing, leaving cliffs and bluffs standing starkly in the glaring sun, browns and reds against a blue sky."

I stopped at a parking lot to rest and look over the silver jewelry for sale; I needed presents for friends. I spoke to the women running the stands but there would be no conversation coming there. I couldn't tell if it was

them or me. I was invisible until I spoke, and many seemed to prefer that I stay invisible. No one wanted a piece of the outsider. Back in Arizona, invisible, the outsider picked up 160 west again, and headed for the Grand Canyon.

Grabbing lunch in Tuba City I got a lot of unfriendly looks, but beyond that was left alone. I was daydreaming on the road out of town when an old man in a weathered pickup looked me squarely in the eye, waited, then pulled out right in front of me. Hitting the brakes hard, I managed to avoid a crash. I was resolved to stay alert, see the canyon, and get off the reservation as soon as possible.

With the score tied 0-0, there were no friends made and no friends lost. "Hasta La Vista!"

15
THE CANYON

There was nothing "painted" about the Painted Desert as I passed by, so I made no stops. Turning onto 64 west at Cameron I approached Grand Canyon, still thirty miles further on, from the north east. The entrance was designated primarily by the abundance of jewelry stands that were not permitted inside.

At Desert View, around a hairpin curve, I got my first good look at the canyon. It was impressive but I was surprised by my lack of enthusiam. It looked pretty much like every postcard I've ever seen of it.

Riding along the south rim, quick glances to the right satisfied my curiosity, but there won't be any stopping. My first priority was to get a campsite.

I'd often wondered why the South rim of the canyon is so busy, while the North rim, while not much harder to reach is relatively quiet. It occured to me as I drive west that the North rim views look directly into the sun, making it more difficult to see. The walls of the south rim are largely hidden in shadow when viewed from the north.

Surprisingly, at the visitor center I had no trouble getting a campsite for two nights. The campground was uninviting, and in the process of pitching the tent, I ripped the zipper. My anger flared and I stormed around for ten minutes before cooling off. It was a pain in the butt, but I'm over-reacting. I'd had a piss poor day up until then and my mood was starting to spill over. The tent is a ten year old Eureka and until now it's never let me down.

The next stop was at the back country office to try and get a permit to hike into the canyon. The best I can do is add my name to a long list of stand-bys. "What are my chances of getting down?" I asked the overloaded ranger.

"Zip-o" he replied without a trace of a smile.

Pandemonium was breaking out on the South Rim. The road was jammed with 'Drive Bys' rushing through on their journeys east or west. I'm amazed and depressed at the sudden transformation. RV's are everywhere, lumbering along the roads with long strings of cars trailing after them. Cars and Busses were buzzing from lookout to lookout. I took the opportunity to drive along the rim and check out the views. I must be the only person ever who was uninspired. I do understand that if I could hike down into the canyon, I'd get a very different impression.

Up ahead an RV did a roll through of a stop sign, and he didn't see me in time. I reacted slowly as the RV slammed on the brakes too late, blocking the lane. Instinct jerked the bike onto the gravel shoulder at forty miles an hour, I bounced past the RV and back onto the road - furious.

Not waiting to put down the kick stand. I laid the bike on its side, jumped up and gave the finger to the RV driver. He didn't see me. He was stopped, still blocking the road; an old man getting his ass reamed out by his wife who seemed madder than I was. The man was as white as a sheet. I put down my hand and sat on the side of the road. The RV drove by without any sign from the occupants that they saw me. I was angry and badly shaken by the day's events and stayed sitting.

As at Mesa Verde, the best time to check the views was in the evening with the rush over. I checked my status at the back country office and learned that I had no real chance of getting down tomorrow either. I considered bailing out, heading north, and blowing off the second day here. I've had nothing but bad feelings and experiences since entering Arizona and I had to shake off this toxic dust.

Driving west into Grand Canyon Village I parked by an inviting old hotel. This was the 'El Tovar' built in 1905 and named after one of Coronado's officers. Here there was more harmony, a sense of history, and I wished I could have landed a room. Across from the hotel was the abandoned rail station.

Journal Entry 1988: One of the developments which brought many more visitors to the south rim of the canyon was the construction of a Santa Fe Railroad spur line from Williams, Arizona. The first train-- Locomotive 282--arrived on September 18, 1901, and trains continued to run to the canyon from 1901 to 1968

SHRINERS STANDING BY 5 STEAM LOCOMOTIVES IN PHOTO.
28 MAR. 1937 NPS PHOTO.
GRAND CANYON NATIONAL PARK MUSEUM COLLECTION,
P.O. BOX 129, GRAND CANYON, AZ 86023

Once a bustling operation, now the tracks are choked with small trees, the platforms crumbling. I appreciate when these relics of the past are left in place and not swept away in an attempt to sanitize the view. Kicking around the old platforms brings deep feelings of nostalgia.

I stood on what was once the farthest platform. It was probably the first to go out of service because the trees were taller there, the tracks obscured by heavy vegitation. Sitting against a tree, a few minutes were spent updating the journal. I woke suddenly on the shaded concrete, without ever realizing that I'd stretched out. People were walking around on the platforms but no one noticed me back in the corner. This had been a relaxing hour, I felt better, but a decision had been reached; I've had enough, tomorrow I'm moving on.

At the store I bought a sewing kit so I could patch up the tent, then sat outside at a picnic table eating my lunch. Nearby, a pair of teenage bikers

had the rapt attention of a couple of young girls as they discussed their exploits. They seemed to be French and I envied them the attention they were getting. It'd been a couple of days since I'd shared anything other than shallow conversations - just exchanging vacant information in a few sentences. I'd love to relax over a beer and enjoy some honest companionship. A chance to talk over my troubles on the reservation this morning would have helped me come to terms. I was still pissed, but understood that my ire would have to be dealt with before it festered. That wasn't going to happen anytime soon.

I'd been across other reservations and felt no animosity, always being treated cordially or with indifference. It was different today and for the time being, I'd need to stay clear of them where possible, or move through quickly on major roads. However sympathetic you might have been to their circumstances mattered not a whit; a lone outsider on a motorcycle was too convenient a target for those with a grudge.

Tourists were still buzzing along the canyon rim when I got back to the campsite, where I botched the job of repairing the zipper. Bad vibes all day, this was just an ugly place for me right then - it happens.

I had the campsite for two nights, but tomorrow I was packing out, maybe turning back. I'd come a respectable distance, seen things that others would never see; turning back now was no disgrace. Maybe it was time. I'd never committed to reaching the Pacific and didn't owe anything to anyone.

Deep inside I knew that line of thinking was a crock. Whatever my rationale for past failure, there were two bottles of Atlantic Ocean in my bags that said otherwise. I wasn't about to let a snap decision haunt me – I had to put the game out of reach. *There was a commitment*, if only to myself and I was going to finish. Grabbing my jacket I got back on the bike.

The ride that evening helped strengthen my resolve. It was a pleasure to drift from lookout to empty lookout with the sun low on the horizon. There were a few short friendly conversations and I got a better impression of the canyon, however my anger was still simmering; there was nothing here to see that would alter my decision to leave.

16
ZION

Eager to go, the bike was packed and warming up just as the sky started to brighten. Roads were empty and the lookouts silent. This was much more of what I wanted, a very different sentiment – the kind that awakens instincts. I felt as if I was in a cathedral with the "Moonlight Sonata" being played.

Without the distraction of bus engines, crowds and honking horns, the canyon regained its majesty.

The sun was coming up fast and I took several haunting photos before moving on toward DesertView and the park's east entrance.

There was no point in staying. I understood that yesterday's pandemonium was only a few hours away and I wanted no part of it. I considered turning west and visiting the North rim - there'd be no crowds on that side. However my mind was made up; I'd already kissed this place goodbye.

Based on the strong recommendation of a friend who long ago passed this way, Zion National Park would be the next stop. In 88 Zion was still relatively unknown, and at that point I hoped for a quieter pace than what I'd just seen at the Grand Canyon and Mesa Verde.

For a long while Zion wasn't regarded as a top tier park. Maybe because its top tier features can't be seen from a car window or at the end of a short brisk walk. While still back in Jersey, I'd done research on Zion and the pictures I'd spotted in old National Geographics were impressive; my hopes were high.

Located at the extreme northern border of Arizona, Page is right at the lower tip of Lake Powell. I gassed up and grabbed breakfast. The lake was formed from the Colorado river when the Glen Canyon Dam was finished in 1966. I'd long wanted to come here, rent a houseboat and spend a week exploring the Lake.

Crossing the dam, the Colorodo river was broad, slow and very blue. Spending several minutes down by the boat ramp I checked out several moored houseboats before moving on.

I was still traveling on 89, heading west, then north again. The air was getting hot but driving was smooth and easy, with just a few slow moving vehicles and plenty of passing opportunities. Driving Utah roads was a real pleasure, with plenty of service stations, food, and rest stops. The scenery was so dramatic - an indescribable sensation on a day like today. The feel of the stiff wind on my face as it rammed hot fragrances into my head was energizing, while the steady throbing of the engine below my feet never stopped.

After filling the tank at a faceless service station, I parked the bike and rested for a while in the shade of a tall red boulder. A lanky young truck driver sauntered over and started a conversation. By nature I'm not a compulsive talker, but that day the floodgates were open. It must have been much the same for him, alone in his rig all day. He seemed to enjoy this companionship with a total stranger, showing me pictures of his Harley Sportster which I complemented. That bike always reminded me of a scrawney dog, but it seemed a good match for the lean frame of my companion.

He pulled out and headed north a good ten minutes before me, but I caught up quickly and gave a honk as I passed. In my mirror I saw his hand extend out the window in a wave. Quickly past, he soon disappeared over the horizon. I was moving on, but from time to time I still wonder about these people.

At Mt Carmel junction I took Rt. 9 west to Zion and by three o'clock I was in a short queue at the park entrance. There was a biker in front of me adorned with a collection of golden crucifixes, his leather jacket embossed with angels and devils. Red script letters across the back identified him as a "Biker for Christ" (whatever that meant). My curiosity burned through the fatigue but there would be no contact. He turned and glanced my way, but my deadpan was frozen, my black shades had nothing to share, and I just gave him a slow nod. I didn't want to be his friend. Soon He rumbled off and it was my turn to talk to the guard.

"Eight dollars please" he said in a slow friendly voice.

"I have a Golden Eagle Pass" I replied. "Let me dig it out".

I was slightly stunned when he told me not to bother. "I trust you. Enjoy the Park!". Hard to articulate how good this made me feel. Those short sentences were a tonic. All the frustration I felt at The Grand Canyon yesterday was washed away.

As always the first objective was to nail down the base camp. The lowdown on Zion said you've got to get off the trail to see the good stuff. I planned to stay here awhile and 'getting off the trail' was exactly what I had in mind.

The torturous road snaked through many hairpin switchbacks, dove deep into multicolored canyons, through dark tunnels, up and over startling ridges. One tunnel, over a mile long curved its way through the side of a mountain. Inside, the cool air was a welcome relief. Every now and again light streamed in through openings to my right. They appeared to be windows, but I could see nothing of the outside in the quick glimpses snatched.

Four bikes heading east passed by. We beeped to each other and the sound bounced off the walls and chased me out the far side. Bang – I was back in the bright light and heat, dropping through more switchbacks into another valley. The colors were brighter than ever and I knew I was going to enjoy this place.

Without stopping to explore, I drove out the park's west gate and chose a campground located about twenty miles further west. Not a terrifically beautiful site, but it had a store, showers, a pool, and best of all only one other occupant - perfect.

Although tired, I zipped back into the park, and stopped at the visitors center. I cornered a ranger and asked her about hiking in the 'Narrows'. She was a big help, and patient with all of my questions. The narrows are often closed to hiking due to the extreme risk of flooding. Storms twenty or thirty miles to the north can cause flash floods, even if the park enjoys full sunshine. She told me there's no rain in sight so it's ok to plan my trip. I grabbed my share of the inevitable park literature for tonight's reading, then split.

I had just enough time to do a quick survey of the Park, so I drove into Zion Canyon. The Virgin river carved the canyon over millions of years and the effect is spectacular, like nothing I've seen so far. I drove the seven miles to the end of the road and parked the bike. There's a sign marking the "Gateway To The Narrows Trail". The sign explained that the native name "Ioo goon" for the canyon means "The place where you come out the way you go in."

The path was paved to allow wheelchair access, so it was very easy going. The roar of the Virgin river grew louder, masking my sounds, and making it easy to photograph deer and other wildlife. The dry trail ended after about a mile, because the river filled the canyon wall to wall. I wasn't prepared to go any further now, but early tomorrow morning this would be my jumping off point. A sign said the danger level was 'HIGH', but not 'EXTREME'. I tried to reconcile that with what the ranger told me an hour ago. I guess 'High Danger' equates to 'It's ok' in her mind.

"Who was that woman?"

There was a quick impulse to stop back for a clarification, but I want to do the hike, and will go with the ranger's advice. "Piss on the sign."

In the end reason prevailed, and I stopped back and asked. It was a different ranger now and he explained in detail: "If you're a strong swimmer and prepared to spend hours hiking in 58 degree water you won't have any problems". The ranger looked at me. "If we expected thunder storms the danger would be

'Extreme' and the river would be closed." He checked

me over. "You should be ok."

'Should be OK' = OK - Two for two – 'OK' it is.

Just beyond the west gate I stopped at a small restaurant for dinner; two cruisers were parked outside, loaded with gear. Inside, the riders were easy to catch, being just as crusty and weathered as myself. They spotted me in a heartbeat, and waved me over. Joining them for dinner was one of the rare treats of the trip. 'Outsiders', they were two Germans traveling east out of LA and heading for the Atlantic. They'd come over a thousand miles and were amazed at the distance I'd traveled (over six thousand miles at that point). For three hours we swapped stories, maps and tips, over dinner and cold beer. We were talking loudly and other patrons chimed in with info and suggestions. They'd have been great road companions, but were leaving in the morning and heading east. I wasn't willing to do that.

It was early evening when I headed west again toward the campsite. I was comfortable there, and decided to extend for a few more days. I wasn't as beat up as I expected but still pretty tired. There was one other occupied campsite, and it belonged to a French geologist who was working on her doctors thesis (a study of the faults in Zion and Bryce Canyons.) Her name was Katrine and she seemed nice, but didn't speak much English. She managed to tell me that she preferred Bryce to Zion, but she's never hiked up the Virgin River. She declined my offer to come along tomorrow. I said goodnight and sacked out.

17
THE NARROWS

Birds began their morning songs, waking me as the sides of my tent started to lighten. There wasn't a scrap of desire to get moving this early, knowing what was in store. However, I was determined to be the first one up the river today, providing an opportunity to photograph without tourists cluttering the foreground. The air was cold and the idea of jumping into 58-degree water held little appeal. However, I forced myself to dress and organize my gear. Approaching the problem one step at a time made it easier; I'd worry about the cold water when I got to the river.

The half hour ride chilled me to the bone, and parking my bike in the empty lot, my enthusiasm was mixed. I briskly walked the trail, hoping to warm up a bit. The sound of rushing water could be heard as soon as the engine stopped, but at the trail head, the rapids were booming. There were no other visitors and the wildlife was taking full advantage of the lull. Deer were everywhere, and I reminded myself to stay alert.

With me were the two older Minolta SRT 101s. One I'd carry on me and the other, wrapped in plastic would serve as a backup. These were mechanically operated models, not as vulnerable to water damage as the newer electronic versions. Both of these cameras had been doused in the past and survived. As long as I got some good pictures, both cameras were expendable. Cameras, lunch, water and film went into the backpack.

A quick check of the register showed that I wasn't the first one in the water after all. There were three names already on the list as I added my own. I decided

to wear my riding boots to protect my feet and ankles. Some lapse of judgment convinced me that I'd be better off without socks.

Everything was ready, now there was nothing left but to do it. Wearing shorts and a heavy wool sweater, with the river roaring in my ears, I waded in and turned upstream. It was 6:30 am.

The cold wasn't as fierce as expected, but as water started to leak into the boots, my feet began to cramp. I knew this would pass as the water warmed up inside. The current was strong, and forcing my way against the belly high stream was harder than I expected. The first job was to hide my valuables; wallet and keys were zipped in a pocket of my leather jacket, then hidden about a hundred yards upstream behind a pile of boulders. At this point, the river was roughly forty feet wide and the walls rose 900 feet above me on either side. The canyon was musty dark and would probably be that way for most of the day. For the next eight hours, my head was filled with the smell of water and the sounds of 'Wassermusik'.

Journal Entry 1988. It was tough going. The footing was tricky in spots and on two occasions, I almost fell, barely managing to hold the camera clear. The river twisted, got shallow, then deeper; in some spots it was impassable, and I was forced to find a way around. I could easily swim it if not for the camera.

Just up ahead, a man and a woman were forcing their way upstream. They found a shallow spot next to the cliff on the inside bend of the river where a large boulder had created an eddy. I slogged in and joined them for a rest. We smiled and shared this quiet moment without feeling the need to speak. All of us were on the same page. They decided to turn back, while I snapped a few shots and

stared at the red walls of the ever-deepening canyon.

Looking up at the thin strip of bright blue sky, I realized that it was full daylight now. Probably getting very warm up there, but none of that heat penetrated down in. I observed birds that I couldn't identify, plummeting, dropping like rocks then pulling out of their dives at the last instant, skimming the water at 8 – 12 inches. I could almost feel their excitement.

Alone in the water I had the chance to reflect on a range of subjects, and in spite of the effort needed to slog upstream, I was very relaxed. I became more proficient at navigating the current. The cascade bounced from side to side, creating areas of slack water that were easy to pass through. In places, especially around long wide turns, the inside bank was dry and firm. I seized these moments to rest. At one of those stops, two young Scots came thrashing upstream, singing loud songs that I'd never heard before (or since). We talked quietly for a moment before they moved upstream while I continued to take pictures.

By 11:30, the river was noticeably more shallow and narrower. I passed several side canyons stretching off into their private gloom, but felt no urge to explore them. Eventually I passed one where the water was only a few inches deep so I headed up. It was surprisingly hard to see in the humid murk.

There had been warnings about quicksand at the park office but they remained forgotten until I found myself waist deep in the stuff. It happened in an instant, a real 'oh shit!' moment, but unlike Hollywood quicksand, I wasn't sucked to the bottom clutching at a vine. It was easy to wade out of, but very difficult, even with the river at my disposal, to get that crap off my clothes.

Back in the main canyon, I kept pushing upstream as the walls got higher, and the river became more constricted. It was impossible to know how far I'd come; I guessed only a few miles, though it felt like twenty. The transition into the "Narrows" proper seemed sudden, and it swallowed my mind. The water was shallow now, a rivulet wandering among sand bars. Walls, which in spots were only eight to ten feet apart, would bend and twist two thousand feet above my head. Alone in this crack, I struggled to catch any glimpse of the sky. I might as well be in a cave. Thirty feet above my head, logs wedged between the walls attested to the reality of flash floods. Not hard to guess what my chances would be in one of those.

By 12:30 I'd seen enough and decided to head back out. I expected the walk to be a long one, but with the river behind me, the distance was covered in half the time, with a few stops to talk to groups working their way in. Always the same question - "How Far is it?" The return was so easy that I relaxed too much, twice falling and soaking the camera. No matter, it would dry in the sun and I had my pictures.

The river flew by and before I knew it, I'd gathered up my jacket and splashed ashore at the trailhead. When I finally pulled off my swollen boots, I was amazed to find my feet covered in blisters. The water was so cold that I never felt them during the hike; but I was feeling them now.

Thirty or forty people congregated at the end of the trail with no intention of going any further. Several tried to engage me in conversation, but I wasn't enthusiastic - answering in monosyllables between mouthfuls of wet sandwich. I didn't mean to be a prick, but I was beat and wasn't ready to share my feelings with strangers. Brimming with the experience, I didn't want to pollute it now with shallow conversation. In three hours I'd be begging for shallow conversation.

When I got back to the campground, it was 110 degrees in the shade. I put the boots in the sun to dry, and put myself in the kiddie pool to soak my blisters.

Some decisions were made in the pool. Death Valley was out. I couldn't imagine how hot it was there; no place for an air-cooled engine or an air-cooled idiot. Los

Angeles is probably out as well. Where I'd hit the coast was still in the air, and that was just as well.

Wanting to try for some overhead vistas of the canyon, I pulled out the maps. The park brochure showed a few trails with possibilities, so I put on my running shoes and limped out again. Driving back through the long tunnel lost nothing for being a repeat experience. The hike was an easy one, but I found myself more fatigued than I thought, and after four or five miles commandeered a cave that got me out of the sun.

In the cool of the cave, I decided to stay at Zion for at least another day. Leaning back against the stone wall, I could see blue sky and multicolor cliffs. I made a supreme effort to capture my feelings of this morning on paper, but had to settle for short lumpy vignettes that would need to be sewn together later.

Compared to last night, dinner was dull and I ate by myself.

Three teenage boys on sports bikes were making a run from Milwaukee to Vegas. They were clearly exhausted and considered staying, but in the end they pushed on. I didn't understand what they thought they'd get from their experience, rushing blindly past the best sights. If they survived, their friends would call it 'Epic'. It really would be an impressive bit of endurance: 'Fear and Loathing' on their own terms. I hope they made it.

At dusk, the campground came alive with the addition of twenty young Germans touring the west. Enjoyable company, I spoke with some of them until dark and then turned in - a long day.

18
BRYCE

Another early start today, driving back through the park again and out the east gate. At the Mt. Pleasant Junction with Route 89, I stopped to fill the tank and took some shit from the attendant when I used the window washing sponge to clean off my tank. He was a two-bit jerk making a 'BFD' over nothing. Normally a guy like this would get my goat, but he wasn't worth the

bother and I kept my mouth shut.

The park was about 60-70 miles away - a pleasant easy ride down long two lane roadways. There was plenty to see and no traffic to contend with.

I stopped for breakfast at a restaurant called "Ruby's". Evidently, Reuben Syrett had set up the first lodge just outside the park entrance and often guided visitors into the canyon. The restaurant was filled with old pictures taken in the 20's and 30's. I wondered if it would please Ruby to see how this restaurant has fossilized him in black and white photography.

Journal Entry 1988: Inside the park I headed straight for the 'Amphitheater'. While there were many attractions, I decided to explore one of the main sites in detail rather than just skim through the park; I only planned to spend one day. The parking lot overlooks a splendid view of the canyon, which was stunning with its deep red brown rocks. Lookouts were crowded and I started to get the same bad feelings that I had at the Grand Canyon. The quick solution (not an option at the GC) was to dive in. I chose a trail that was about eight miles long and started down. Even the trails were crowded for a while. Many of those people were very out of shape and would have their work cut out climbing back up.

Beyond the first mile the trails emptied and there was no one to bother me."

The park was a study in vivid contrasts. Rocks were deep red, with scattered dark green Spruce; Ponderosa and Western Yellow Pine highlighted against them. Overhead the sky was a cloudless deep blue.

Bryce Canyon was unique. Many of the rock formations, called Hoodoos remind me of 'drip castles' that I'd made at the beach as a kid. Mule deer and small varmints were everywhere. Dust was fine, easy to kick up, and before long I was covered in it, streaking my face with sweat.

From time to time I'd pass people moving in the opposite direction. Just a wave with no conversation - ships passing in the night. The scenery was uniformly beautiful but unvaried."

There were plenty of opportunities for photography but I was getting bored and picked up the pace. About a mile out, crowds reappeared.

Climbing out was easier than expected, and I spent a while at the top just gazing over the rim. I was becoming saturated with natural wonders, and wasn't fully appreciating or digesting everything I'd seen.

I left the park and on the ride back to Zion decided to push on to California. It was a leisurely ride back to

camp. At one point I had to wait as cattle were herded onto the road, slowly flowing through the same narrow pass that I needed to use. I smiled broadly at a cowgirl high above me on her horse. She must have thought I was mocking her and I got a scowl in return. God knows what kind of crap she must take from motorists.

The road finally cleared and I ripped along for most of the way. One final ride through the tunnel, then it was back to camp.

I ate a light dinner at the picnic table. I'd gotten to know Larry the campground owner and he stopped by to talk for a while. Guessing that he envied my apparent freedom, I didn't confide that my determination was wavering. Zion & Bryce had recharged the batteries, but I knew that there'd better be no long delays reaching the coast. Once the crossing was completed, I could relax and re-access.

Then there was a long talk with Katrine, who spoke more English than she first let on, mostly about travel in France. I got to bed late, for once with no pressing schedule. It was time to move on; but I could sleep in tomorrow.

19
THE WAVES OF NEVADA

It was a relatively late start by most days' standards. At 8:30 I was on my way heading west out of the campground. The road followed the Virgin River, which supported a thin strip of greenery in an ocean of browns and reds. After weeks of roaming dry barrens, the fresh smell of river water was a welcome change that would be missed later in the day.

The road wound twenty miles, on through Rockville, without much change in the scenery. The high bluffs north of the road were lit by early morning sun, displaying all of their colors. The cool sweet air reminded me of early autumn, bittersweet memories of the first days of school.

At La Virken, I turned north for a few miles to the interstate.

Journal Entry 1988: The Interstates, when I used them, were viewed as something akin to "Worm Holes". They transported me at high speed from one portal on to the next, the bike appearing suddenly out of grasslands, and then once again vanishing down an empty canyon.

In other accounts of motorcycle trips there's a sense, if not stated specifically, that highways are to be shunned. At the start of this trip, that was my intention. However, the road transformed me, and early prejudices gave way. Driving an empty Interstate on a beautiful morning with stunning scenery was a welcome change of pace. Long days trapped behind crawling RV's, or spent edging past cattle on the open range has dimmed the romance of back roads. On highways I felt like I was fast-forwarding through whole chapters of stuff I've already seen.

I-15 took me north for about thirty minutes to Cedar City. I liked the sound of that name and could almost smell it - but just like Big Timber in Montana, Cedar City was just one more generic exit.

Now the road turned west on route 56 into Nevada. The land was dry and nondescript, lacking the stark beauty of Utah and it made no lasting impression. There was a divergence at a sign for "The Mountain Meadow Massacre." Today, the site is just a quiet

shallow alpine valley, sharing its peaceful beauty with anyone who goes to the trouble of visiting.

At the time, I didn't know much about the incident. A wagon train of settlers heading west was massacred at the hands of white settlers who attempted to place the blame on the indigenous tribes. It's not my intention to detail it here, and easy enough to research if interested. I will say that it wasn't a proud moment for those groups involved.

I was wary about Nevada. The maps showed very few towns along the planned route so I stopped at Panaca to gas up outside of a featureless bar. Horses were tied up out back. Before I started this trip, I knew I had to stay out of places like this unless I wanted to get the shit kicked out of me. I filled the tank to the gills and waited a few minutes for an attendant before noticing the sign. "Pay for gas at the bar", my fate was sealed.

Journal Entry 1988: It was hot inside and smelled of old wood and beer. My eyes took a moment to adjust.

There was nobody at the register, so I waved to the bartender who was serving three men at the far end. They had dark button down work shirts and all of them were wearing chaps. It must be their horses tied up out back.

One of them was walking over so I included him in the next question. "How far to the next gas?" They weren't sure.

"You might have to get to Tonopah. They have plenty there." They assured me that the route I had planned was my best bet, so I stuck with my plan.

Then, while staring at my riding chaps, he asked "Do you think yours would do a better job of keeping out prickly pear cactus than mine?"

His chaps were well-worn brown leather, with traditional trimmings that were in various stages of decomposition. "Don't think so. Yours look thicker than mine."

The situation I'd dreaded, turned out to be a welcome interlude. The other two guys had wandered over and started talking. They'd been on the herd half the night, and were tired of talking to each other. I ordered up three more beers for them. The older of the men told the bartender to make it four.

It seemed like all morning, but was less than an hour. We talked, and asked questions. I carefully echoed their opinions, while nursing that one beer. They had work left and were doing the same. At one point, we tried on each other's chaps. I fought down an impulse to offer up a swap. I wanted them, but had no place to pack an extra pair, and was not about to wear them. All I needed was to pass a pack of "Mongols" wearing cowboy chaps.

The youngest of the three was an amateur historian,

and he knew his stuff. We spoke briefly about Gettysburg before discussing the impact on the American Revolution, of the death of George Augustus Howe - shot dead in a skirmish outside of Ticonderoga. That I knew the land around the fort like the back of my hand seemed to garner his esteem.

I was thinking through an exit strategy, when the older man got up and shook my hand. "We got work to do. Nice talking to you." They all left through the back door, and just like that, it was over and the bar was empty. Did those men find my drifting in to be odd? Or was I just the latest roadshow to pop in at lunchtime? Later I kicked myself for not taking any pictures, but they may not have wanted me to. Those guys were the real thing. Back on the road, I passed through Caliente and a bunch of other unnamed towns.

The "Extraterrestrial Highway" was simply Route 375 back in 88, passing quietly by the unknown and invisible "Area 51". Heading northwest, the land was coming at me in waves. Every ten miles there was a ridgeline followed by a long flat plain. The head in my helmet was mesmerized by the heat, monotonous scenery and the constant drone of the engine. A change in the pitch of the engine as it labored up the next ridge would snap me out of it. I'd hit the throttle, charge up the ridge, and then drift down the far slope onto the next plain. It became the pattern for several hours, as the gas needle continued its migration toward 'E'.

I'd never make Tonopah – that much was clear. I had enough gas to turn around, but there were no better routes. It was time to trust my luck.

In this vast desert, I pulled over to ask a guy, standing by his mailbox, if there might be gas at Warm Springs. I could just make that, but he didn't know.

Historical Note: *The following year, 1989, a local resident named Bob Lazar would ignite a firestorm by claiming to have worked on alien spacecraft inside 'Area 51'. As Lazar was the only resident for forty miles along this lonely stretch, I've sometimes wondered who it was that I spoke with. Had I been at the famous 'Black Mailbox'?*

At Rachael, I stopped to let the engine and the oil cool off. What town there was featured a small store where I grabbed a sandwich, but there wasn't a scrap of shade to sit under. Staying inside, the storeowner assured me that "there's no gas at Warm Springs anymore. Why don't you just fill up here? I have pumps out back." Feeling the tight muscles in my neck start to unknot, I wanted to tell him "You'll sell more gas if you put up a *FUCKING SIGN*".

I would have driven off and run dry forty miles short of Tonopah. Walking out the front door, I picked up on the large sign out front, and was glad that for once I'd kept my dumb mouth shut. How'd I miss it?

Green pastures and distant valleys called out to me from across the road to the east. Dirt roads wandered off into the hills beyond. I toyed with the idea of riding off that way but shook the impulse quickly. There was enough trouble keeping fueled on the highways.

Journal Entry 1988: As the journey continued, it occurred to me that I've no idea whether it was July or August and could care less. My route turned west at Warm Springs, which was hardly worthy of a name. There's no gas. Filling the tank would come at Tonopah along with a burger. The name is familiar, an old song maybe. I think it was Linda Ronstadt but I don't recall for sure.

West of Tonopah, there was a low hot stretch of prairie before starting the climb into the Sierra foothills. I wondered if this depression was an extension of "Death Valley" which is a bit further north. Dust devils were forming in the valley behind. They were fascinating to watch but trying to photograph them was a fruitless effort.

Up ahead was the California state line, and in the pass just beyond was the agricultural checkpoint. A young man waved me into the line, and annoyed, I complied. A moment later an older guy motioned me ahead with the comment "what the hell is he thinking?" I moved along with a shrug.

Grinding up a badly worn county road that ran just east of the Sierra's, took up my last mental reserves. Like central Nevada, the land is coming at me in waves. But this time they are short, steep, and frequent. In the journal, I referred to them as "pops", because that's how they felt on the bike. Mono Lake was my destination. I'd find a place to pitch off-road in the Lundy Lake

region, and then explore the park.

Mono Lake was relatively unknown at the time, and it's doubtful that I'd have gone far out of my way to see it; just a simple coincidence, located adjacent to the east entrance of Yosemite. The lake proved well worth my time.

Historical Note: Mono Lake is fed by streams and a large number of mineral springs. Over the centuries, calcium and other minerals from the springs have built up, layer by layer, into impressive columns called tufas. In the 1940's, the City of Los Angeles taped the lake as part of its water supply. They took more than the lake could replenish, particularly when there was little snow. Over the decades, the level of the lake dropped twenty or more feet, exposing the tufas. Local resistance mounted, and in the 1990's, court decisions ended the practice of draining the lake. Water levels are up and will continue to rise, once again hiding these dramatic structures.

Journal Entry 1988: I haven't done the totals yet, but this has probably been the longest day in terms of miles. Sleep came as soon as my head hit the rolled up towel.

Yosemite Falls

20
YOSEMITE

<u>Journal Entry 1988</u>: *The predawn glow was all I had to help me pull down the tent. I was up early trying to beat the crowds into Yosemite Valley. Arguably, the most physically beautiful place in the US, there'll be no escaping the mobs today.*

The morning was cool and I ate quickly at the diner, before leaving the town of Lee Vining behind forever. The rising sun was just starting to catch the tree tops as the bike started the long climb up to Tioga Pass."

Geographical Note: At over *9000 feet high, Tioga Pass is the highest drivable pass in the Sierra Nevada Range. The road is only open seasonally with extended closure during the winter months.*

The eastern slope was rocky, and vegetation sparse, with no trace of lingering snow. In summer, State Highway 120 is the eastern entrance to Yosemite, but the valley was a long ride from Lee Vining.

My route climbed with occasional switchbacks, and again the engine struggled at altitude as the combustion process fought for air. Ahead, a long line of cars was stuck behind an RV grinding its way up the slope. Before long, a line formed behind me as well. There were plenty of opportunities for him to pull over and let us pass, but he wouldn't do it. What a jerk.

Finally reaching the crest, I started down, passing several trailheads along the way. The west slope gets more rain, was heavily forested and quite a bit steeper.

Traffic increased as we descended and my hands were constantly working clutch and brake. By the junction of Big Oak Flat, the road was bumper to bumper. This wasn't going to work and I was ready to keep driving, but catching a glimpse of Bridal Veil Falls, I decided to stick it out. As long as I was here, there was no sense in not stopping. I was well aware there would be no miracle as at Yellowstone. At the valley entrance we were all inching along in fits and starts.

It took almost an hour to cover the few miles to Yosemite Village. I checked for campsites, and rooms at the Ahwahnee lodge. There were no open campsites. Rooms in the lodge were going for almost $300, and that wasn't happening. I left the bike parked at the lodge and walked, getting views of El Capitan, half dome, and Yosemite falls. Snagging a crappy room outside the park wouldn't cut it for me either; this is far worse than Grand Canyon. It's time to keep driving.

I left the park via the Mariposa exit, and stopped at the Park gate to ask directions.

"Where you headed Jersey Plates? "

"I *was* headed here."

"Too crowded?"

Just shook my head.

A derelict cog rail bed and an old wooden building, formerly the station, justified a stop. In the days before roads came to the park, the railroad brought in supplies for those brave and fit enough to hike in. The building had retained its character, offering a glimpse of the old 'Golden State' and the quality of its people.

Back on the road, the temperature in the Central Valley was well into the mid 90's. There was a lot of agriculture, and the unchanging scenery made the ride seem endless.

I reached I-5 at Merced, stopping for fast food more for the AC than anything they can offer me to eat. The place was mobbed with moms and kids in strollers, everyone roaring in and roaring out, a paradigm of Yosemite.

Here was a decision point again, and I have two big ones to deal with. First, there are friends to be seen in LA; friends who expect to hear from me along the way. I did plenty of corporate duty in Southern California and have already seen much of what lies between there and Frisco. The final decision is made; there will be no rehashing old ground, there is little love lost between me and Los Angeles.

The second choice, where to reach the coast, has to be considered. I'd stopped denying that this was anything other than an ocean-to-ocean trip. Assuming California to be the best place to 'splash-in', I'd never given it any serious thought. Now I wasn't so sure.

Over Big Macs I poured over small maps. I could hit the coast north of Frisco and follow it up to Oregon; that was all new ground. However, it was too far west; there was no good way to come back for Crater Lake and Mt St. Helens. (This was dead wrong, but so what? It's not as if being 'dead wrong' was something new for me.) So there it was; pound up the central valley to Crater Lake and beyond; but to answer the big question – I'll reach the Pacific in Oregon, somewhere north of Coos Bay.

Journal Entry 1988: Back on the interstate it was a long, hot, crowded drive, with nothing remotely enjoyable or noteworthy about this stretch. The miles grind away beneath my feet; the roar of the engine fills my head, but the road rolls on forever. Sacramento drifted away in the mirrors amid vineyards, and fields. My nose filled with the smell of plums, raisins, dust and hot asphalt. An hour north of Sacramento I called it quits at a roadside KOA. The campground was a frying pan, with no trees or shelter - at least there were showers.

I'd come a long way today, but saw nothing that would justify the effort. Zion had been a shot in the arm; my energy and interests aroused again. Long days of hot driving with little gained beyond mileage, consumed much of the new vitality.

21
THE GREY PACIFIC

The cool predawn air would have been stimulating, but any sense of tranquility evaporated under the ceaseless buzzing from the highway. In the last seventy years, we've been transformed from a horse drawn society, to one so permeated with noise that it seems normal. Engines, motors, shrill howls from pitch men, and the pitter-patter of the entertainment industry fill all the empty spaces. People today can live out their lives without ever experiencing the joy of silence. I find no joy in noise.

There were still a few hours of driving north on the Interstate before I could switch to back roads. The highway was busy early, so this must have been a weekday. For once, there was a clear radio signal and I listened to music for a few hours until the signal vanished as I approached the northern peaks. (So much for my rant about noise. Sometimes there's too much silence.)

On the horizon, high peaks became visible in the clear morning air, standing in sharp relief against a dark blue sky. Chief among them was Mt Shasta, which rose slowly from the ground until it dominated the view ahead. The highway, which had been ruler straight, now twisted to find the easiest route through the foothills. Compressed down to two lanes, the roadway would soon be restricted to one lane by the construction crews trying to carve out a broader passage through the canyons. They had their work cut out.

At a fuel stop, my air filter came off again, anticipating higher altitudes. The road was filled with families heading out on vacation; their cars piled high with boats and bikes. It might be Friday, but I've lost track. Days of the week have no meaning beyond campsites being full or campsites being available. There was a long line to get into the Mt Shasta parking lot, so I kept moving on.

In hindsight, I clearly should have spent more time in Northern California; it would prove to be an opportunity squandered, and unfortunately, a mistake

I'd repeat. I was burning out quickly. Setting up a base camp and finding a quiet corner to hole up for a few days would have refreshed my spirits. However, the call of the sea was all I could hear at this point - "Finish what you started." There would be a stop or two, but

after that, I'd be hell bent for the Pacific.

Just north of Shasta, I switched to local roads again, heading northeast on Rt. 97. This was beautiful country and a good road again, a pleasure to drive.

Klamath Falls, well off the Interstates, seemed to be just another town lost in time. It was a busy place but it rang true to childhood memories of the 1950's. Riding out on Route 62, Upper Klamath Lake stretched out on my left for many miles. This seemed a good town to live in, probably the first place where I could see myself staying. The lake itself could take a week to explore in a kayak, and I made a mental note.

Crater Lake was on the radar now, the road was climbing and snow covered the peaks ahead.

At first, the temperature change was welcome but

before long I needed to put on the leathers and gloves, fearful that it might get colder than I'm equipped to handle. In the middle of this hot dry summer (Yellowstone is well on fire by now), there's still snow at Crater Lake. I had to wonder if it ever melts; at least the roads were clear.

I had only a vague idea what to expect, perhaps fuzzy memories of postcards or images from a picture book.

Nobody checked my pass at the entrance, and the parking lot was empty. There was a short walk over a low, rocky rise and the scene confronted me all at once. Even after all these years, and all the trips I've taken, it's hard to imagine a more strikingly beautiful view. The visual equal of Yosemite, it wins the tiebreaker hands down by the complete absence of gringos, dingoes, and ticking engines. With my head still saturated with Utah's dramatic, but dead canyons and bluffs, Crater Lake would stir my soul.

A desperately chatty ranger appeared out of nowhere and found her guy, filling me up with as much information as I could absorb. Warmed by that young woman's enthusiasm, I asked about camping. There were sites available, but she warned that even though the air was comfortable now, it would be very cold tonight with snow a possibility. The surrounding drifts reinforced that message, and spending the night is forgotten. I'd be warm enough in the tent, but had no desire to ride snow covered roads tomorrow.

Sprawled on a rock that had been warming in the sun, it was only a matter of time before I was asleep. Thirty minutes later, nothing had changed. The ranger was still hovering in the vicinity, hoping for someone to talk to. Most of the hiking trails were still buried in snow and there was little point in staying here other than to enjoy the view. I had the urge to move on, and after making a few notes in the journal, it was time to go.

Mount Saint Helens had been on the list of places to visit since day one, but it too became a victim of my march to the sea. The biggest mistake I'd make; it's one

I still bitterly regret. In 1988 the scars of the eruption were still plain to see, and would have been endlessly fascinating, bringing to life the enormous drama of the 1980 eruption. The opportunity was squandered, lost forever; it's impossible to calculate where the trip would have headed from there. Several days spent at that base camp would have been energizing in the extreme.

Instead, I'd wend my way up along route 62 and continue north, crossing the pass between walls of compacted snow. From there it was an incredible, hour long glide down into the warm forests north west of Crater Lake; where small inviting towns called out to me to drop anchor for the night. Continuing west, I passed under I-5 at Roseburg without a thought.

Gassing up at a small filling station in Melrose, a friendly man welcomed me to Oregon and the Willamette Valley.

It was an opportune conversation that I was in no hurry to end. He gave directions to Coos Bay, still a good distance to the west. A firm handshake and he was gone, but there's still a warm and lasting impression.

It's proven impossible to reconstruct the roads I followed from Melrose. They were well paved, and very scenic as they took the plunge down to sea level. I followed a small group of three cars that were moving at a good clip, and there was no desire other than to tuck in behind and follow.

This was Pacific Northwest weather now, with patchy fog and heavy storms roaming around. The rumbles of thunder added an ominous note, a sense of impending doom; but for me they didn't materialize until late that evening.

Coos Bay didn't make much of an impression as I rolled in during an evening fog. There wasn't much to see beyond strip malls and stoplights, but I grabbed a hotel room and dug in.

For the first time since Yellowstone, I was holed up under a roof.

22
"PERSEVERANCE FURTHERS"

Journal entries were few and far between now - just occasional jottings. Clothing had been weeded down to the bare minimum: one pair of jeans, a few t-shirts, socks, shorts and a sweater. There's also one pair of nylon running shorts that I bought along the way to wear when everything gets washed. All else has been tossed or shipped home long ago.

That day the crossing was completed; a day that had been on my mind for a long while. I rummaged through the clothes and found a dingy white shirt, then packed out of the hotel.

Coos Bay in the morning sun was cheerful and bustling with an overpowering smell of wet lumber. It was clearly a shipping point for wood products, and I passed mountains of sawdust and wood chips, ready to be loaded into waiting ships or rail cars.

A few miles beyond the motel, the ocean was visible. I passed miles of beachfront campsites; an inviting thought, but it's far too early in the day to grab one. The morning was cool and bright, the road was

empty and I preferred riding to stopping. Rolling due north on the Oregon Coast Highway was some of the best riding of the trip. The views were inspiring, a great change from long weeks of dry canyons.

I still had the two bottles of Atlantic Ocean at the bottom of my saddle bags (this was a real 'leap of faith' because I hadn't seen them in a very long while). I just needed to find the right place to dump them in. I'd often thought about buying a bottle of Champagne, and involving strangers to participate by asking them to

take a picture. Suddenly understanding that this needed to be a private affair, I didn't want to share this with anyone else. Not being in the same space as others just then, I wouldn't risk polluting the experience.

Late in the morning the bike was parked, the tide was out, and the beach extended along the base of tall cliffs. Thanks to calm low water, a short stretch of sand and stone was exposed that I could walk. I don't recall how far along, but a cave appeared at the foot of the cliffs. I had no light with me and couldn't see how deep it ran.

Carved out by the tides, the cave was inundated most of the day. A large rock at the entrance with a hollow depression on top grabbed my attention; without thinking, I dumped both bottles of Atlantic

Ocean into that shallow basin, moved deeper into the cave and sat. There was a lot on my mind and it all seemed to be demanding immediate action. The habits of the last few months were hard to suppress but there was absolutely nowhere I now had to be. Plans didn't need to allow for a path to the sea anymore; a weight had been lifted. I took a deep breath and let it all go. 'Finished'...the word seemed to hang in the air. The

journey was completed and nothing else seemed to matter. I could go or come as I pleased. The oceans would unite. It would take a few hours and I wouldn't be here to see it, but this was a better, more spiritual way for me. Letting the sea take the gift on its own terms seemed far more appropriate than just dumping it in.

I thought back to the times when I wavered. Those first few days of heavy rain almost did me in. Turning back at the Grand Canyon after that horrible sequence would have still made for a respectable trip, but I knew those last sixteen hundred miles would forever trouble me. That didn't happen - Irish stubbornness took control, and instead I just kept pushing west. Well past the point of wanting to see something new, this was all about seeing it through.

I could have finished things off on the California coast a whole lot sooner, and in some respects I'm still surprised that it didn't happen that way. The reward for me was stumbling upon this unique setting, a private chapel in a cliff on the beach; I can't imagine a more fitting end.

The cave held me for about an hour, and the sea had crept back in, reducing the open stretch. I scrambled back to the parking lot, deeply lost in the moment.

Much of the afternoon was spent running the coastal highway north. Stopping for a burger in a small town whose name I didn't bother to record, a guy standing in line behind me wanted to start a conversation and I was more than happy to oblige. With my filthy leathers, it's obvious I was riding.

"Those your Jersey plates?"

I nodded. "Just made the coast today."

"How's the bike holding up. Need anything?"

That seemed like an odd question and it must have shown on my face. "I've been on the same oil since Durango and its been pushed hard - fried a few times."

"That's my shop across the street. I can get you up right now. We can eat over there."

That's how I spent my afternoon: working the bike, re-living the crossing, and laughing down a couple of beers. It all felt so different now. I'd had my private ritual and then found someone to share it with.

The wind was blowing hard on the Columbia River

and I was nervous. The Astoria Bridge was high above the water and fully exposed to the wind. I was dreading open grate roadway which moves a bike from side to side, making it very uncomfortable to control, especially in a cross wind. I don't mind heights, but don't like being able to see the river through the road.

At the toll both, the man warned me to take it easy because the wind was blowing hard.

"What's the road surface up top, paved or open grate?"

"Iron grate. Take it easy."

I drove up the approach sweating out the crossing, got to the top and the bridge was paved from end to end. I didn't know what to think. Was the guy really that stupid or just being a prick?

North of the bridge, I stopped at a hotel near Raymond. There were no rooms available, but I was welcome to pitch my tent on the lawn.

23
BLESSINGS FROM HEAVEN

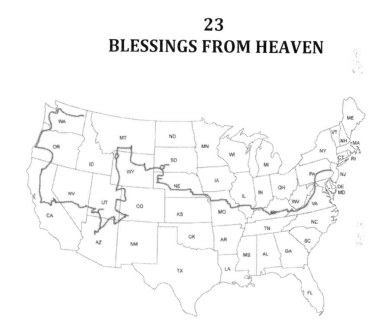

Dawn was cold and damp as I tore down the tent. Dense fog would make driving difficult, and I reconsidered my earlier decision not to install road lights and red rear flashers - maybe a bad call. Hard to tell in the fog, but there seems to be little of note as I work my way north. Olympic National park has been on the agenda for a while, but in this weather it would just be a long ride in a foggy rain forest – no thanks, keep moving.

The outskirts of Seattle were a blur of congestion, as cars and trucks tried to fight their way downtown. The intersection with I-90 was a great relief. The road was empty and it felt good to let the engine run free. Ahead the Cascades, that great volcanic barrier of the Pacific Northwest, blocked the way - its mountains rose up like walls before me. With the low overcast, it was impossible to see a way through. Hard to imagine how the great railroad tycoons, could have envisioned blasting a rail line through this wilderness.

At an exit in the foothills, I took the opportunity to fuel up, filling the tank right up to the bung. It was a long climb to the top; steep grades switching endlessly across the slopes, and finally crossing at Snoqualmie Pass. There were long miles of descents ahead as the bike crested and started down. I could still head south to Mt St Helens and Craters of The Moon. Thoughts of the hot road ahead filled my helmet, choices to make, and roads to take, when abruptly, the engine died.

There was a sudden hard drag, as gears quickly slowed the bike. I pulled the clutch lever and the bike picked up speed on the steep slope. Now what? The road was bottoming out ahead of the next steep climb, and there was no more time. Ready to try anything, I pulled back on the throttle, and let the clutch out, the bike slowed, and then surged ahead as the engine roared up the next steep slope. "What the fuck was that?"

There was an exit with a station ahead, but things seemed ok again; the engine was turning smoothly - keep going.

It took a while to clear the mountains, but by midmorning the Cascades filled my mirrors. The bike drifted onto the hot dry plains of central Washington and plowed along. Hour after hour, fields and orchards flew by. The mercury was topping 100 and the speedometer about the same. I stopped for gas and let the engine shed some of the heat. The rear cylinder in particular was taking a beating. With the oil temperature right at the red mark, the only cooling the engine was getting was the quick fuel/air spray from the carb – not enough. I should have put on an oil cooler, or better yet, used a water-cooled bike.

Thirty minutes in the shade and the engine was still hot, but I couldn't wait there all day. The engine started up and rode well for ten minutes, then quit again. It started up using the same technique, but something was definitely wrong.

With the engine dying at ever shortening intervals, it was a long afternoon fighting my way across the state. Clearly, heading south was out; I had to find a town with a shop. Somewhere along the way, I was served up lemonade at a counter by a young woman who wouldn't talk to or look at me; I didn't exist. A 'helmet dream'? When did it happen?

On the approach to Spokane, the engine was barely alive, bucking, stalling, then roaring to life again for twenty or thirty seconds. It was 5:30 on a Saturday. There would be shops in this town, but would anybody be open, or did I need to wait until Monday; and where do I crash until then?

Traffic had picked up and I was blocking the right lane. Motorists were passing me because clearly the bike was in trouble. I refused to lean into the upcoming tight turn for fear of stalling and going down. My attention was fully occupied with keeping the bike moving and upright. As I eased out of that turn, I glanced at the road ahead; and there it was, a blessing from heaven sitting up above the highway. - "YAMAHA"

I was still hooting a mile later at the exit ramp; from here the bike could be pushed if need be. Not sure where to go, I made the first right and kept driving; couldn't afford to get lost now.

I will always believe he was put there to help me. Ahead, parked on the side having a smoke, a biker watched me jerk my way up the road. After giving me directions, he handed me his card, shook my hand and told me I had a place to stay if I needed one. His name was Monty, never will forget that guy.

The second right got me to the big dealership and it was in the process of closing. Many heads turned at the congested barking of my bike lurching across the parking lot. A motorcycle safety class had run late, but was wrapping up. I approached a salesman who told me they were closing up until Monday; but then the shop owner walked over, looked at the plates, and without another question, the bike was on a lift.

With perseverance, anything that can go right often does.

The owner, his name was Doug, told me the mechanic delayed his plans to get this started, but didn't think it would be done tonight. Now the questions began and a bunch of guys were standing around talking. All of them had toured, and they were always looking for good places to go next, tips, and opinions. I was a wealth of first hand information dropping out of the sky.

The mechanic walked over and told me I couldn't have "squeezed more snot into the carb with a compressor". It'd be ready tomorrow. This guy was going to come in on Sunday to get me rolling. But for tonight, they'd take me across the highway to the hotel. "Could they take me to dinner?"

It felt like a debriefing. Riders who had all toured extensively, shared their experiences, and it was great to just listen and laugh. For one night, I was back inside. Still a few thousand miles of hard riding left but this was the unforeseen end of the odyssey.

NPS Photo (Jim McCowan)

24
COMING IN

A mechanic picked me up at the hotel, and drove me to the shop. The bike was out front. I started it, half expecting the congested rumble that had become such a familiar part of my days. But now it purred'

"It hasn't sounded like this in a long time", I told the Mechanic. There was an uncomfortable moment for me, because I truly didn't have the words to thank them. I shook everyone's hand and left; driving out the same way I'd lurched in yesterday, half expecting Monty to still be standing alongside the road.

Ahead lay a long day on I-90. After crossing Idaho, I chose a second visit to the Custer Battlefield over Glacier National Park. Last time I'd wanted to spend the night there but was forced to leave early because of tire problems. I expected Custer to be busy, but the parts of the battlefield I wanted to explore, were of little interest to most, and would be empty. Glacier is a great Park, but in late summer, it would be crammed with visitors, and I already knew how I'd react to that.

Montana was buzzed by an empty helmet riding a hot engine, roaring along I-90 at 85 to 90 mph. When I started to pick up road signs for Missoula, an old song, "Miss you so badly" filled my helmet and got stuck. Still, I've had far worse things to contend with than some classic Jimmy Buffet banging around.

Just past Missoula the speedometer cable broke and I didn't know how fast I was moving, but 'moving' was the operative word. Rumors of the 'no posted speed limit in Montana' were good enough for me. North of Butte, I could see a haze on the horizon that continued to darken until I lost it at Livingston, where I'd turned south on the ride out. It never entered my clogged mind that Yellowstone was in flames, the worst blaze in recorded Park Service history. I wouldn't pick up on it until I got home and turned on the news.

Twenty miles west of Billings, I paid ten bucks for a room at a "Bates" motel. I'd be at the Custer Battlefield early next morning.

Another beautiful morning ride ended in disappointment. The park road at the battlefield was being repaved, and couldn't be used. Last stand hill was accessible, but I've had enough of that. The campground was full. I left via Rt. 212 a two lane back road that ran north of the battlefield for many miles, eventually back into South Dakota at Belle Fourche. Twenty minutes to the south at Spearfish, I was back on I 90 heading East. I passed 'Harley Heaven' in Sturgis and immediately started picking up 'Wall Drug' signs. It had to be nearly a hundred miles to the Wall exit! It felt like years had passed since I last saw them.

The heat was crushing - 115 in the shade. Every 90 minutes I stopped for gas, water, and thirty minutes of cooling for the engine.

Heat was always the real problem. Both the heat of a western summer day and the heat thrown off an air-cooled engine that's being pushed to its limits.

It was getting dark when I finally grabbed a small cube of a room in Plankinton, SD. A quiet meal at a small diner where everybody was a stranger, lost in their own scripts. The counter was filled with loners, no couples, and no families.

I was on the road before sunrise and there wasn't a shred of exploration left in the plan or in my heart; it was all about getting back. That was another day of brutal driving in the heat; simply moving east, chugging from one pit stop to the next, across South Dakota, and then Minnesota.

Crossing the Mississippi into Wisconsin felt like walking in the front door. The landscape was green, wooded, and smelled of vegetation, life. It seemed to be Sunday, the road filled with families coming back from weekend adventures. I would touch down in two more days.

Monday morning found me snarled in traffic. It took hours to shake free of Chicago's bumper-to-bumper madness. The journal was buried in the bags and the entries had stopped at Spokane. Memories of the return ride were just a series of snippets that caught my eye and stuck.

Further south I took a break at a rest stop Burger King for breakfast. A woman at the next table was conducting a job interview with a young man. I heard a discussion about 'punctuality bonus' and my head popped up. The long arm of Mars Incorporated was about to reel me back in. My employer of twenty years, I'd completely forgotten about them for several months, but now it was time to start thinking about it again. I waited outside, and then spoke with her for a short while before sailing off. It all still seems so very odd.

My recollection of Indiana was three troopers slugging it out with some guy at a tollbooth. Jersey plates had lost their power as the roads and terrain became increasingly familiar. At another rest stop, I spoke briefly with guys from a Harley club who approached me. They thought it looked like I'd been on the road for a while. It was no different in Ohio. I only remember leaving - crossing into Pennsylvania.

There were serious thoughts about pushing on, making it home late tonight with one big push. Nevertheless, as much as I wanted to get home, there was an unexpected reluctance to end the trip.

I don't believe that people change. Instead, they're transformed gradually by the sum of their experiences and learning. They grow or they wither. Some episodes have been far richer than others, and this trip surely was one of those times. I didn't want to end it in a final spasm of compulsive driving.

As each day brought me closer, I could feel the changes - the weight of the road lifting. Stage by stage I seemed to be waking from a dream; a dream that was becoming increasingly remote. The final leg was essential; I wanted to complete the journey awake, aware and appreciative.

My patience was rewarded by a beautiful clear, cool morning. The road was empty and there was time to reflect.

While the trip was never transcendental, it was always very real, very immediate, and unforgettable. Thinking back to the other riders that I met, it seemed the same for them as well. They were all worn down with fatigue and loneliness, while at the same time brimming over with confidence and satisfaction.

Pulling into the driveway and facing the garage door, it seemed a lifetime since I rolled out on that cold rainy morning, timid, wondering what I'd find.

Now I know - and my words fail me.

"I shall be telling this with a sigh
Somewhere ages and ages hence;
Two roads diverged in a wood, and I –
I took the one less traveled by,
And that has made all the difference.

Robert Frost 'The Road Not Taken'

Epilogue

For those who thought I'd never return, they were wrong; I always suspected I would. There was also no transformation in the radical sense. We do become the sum of our experiences; for me the daily exposure to a range of new and beautiful landscapes, sad and lonely situations, and unexpected friendship, opened up a greatly expanded worldview. I met people who were open and friendly, others were hollow and hostile.

I became saturated with new vistas to the point where I couldn't appreciate them anymore. When it became clear to me that this was the case, it was time to come home; still the same guy I've always been, but with a new confidence that would carry me on, through a series of adventures, taking me further and further afield.

There would be kayaking off the Alaskan Coast, and in the Coral Sea, trekking on four continents including the Himalayas, and the Australian rain forest. In 1991, I joined a group of mountain bikers that were following the Old Silk Road across central Asia, from the Soviet Union, across and into China. We were the first to ever do it, but that was the least important aspect of the trip - a trivial coincidence. The journal from that trip will be published next if and when I have the time; because with four kids there's so little of it, and I won't be giving up any time with them.

The Yamaha, my partner in all of this, was fried but it never let me down. When I think back on all those scorching miles with the air filter off, the bikes reliability was amazing.

It's always easy to look back on your life and pick out the key moments. Moments that changed everything and set you on a new course, moments where you grew, or withered. Usually I see them coming, understand their significance, but ignore the consequences. I don't know - it's kind of who I am.

This trip was an exception. I knew it would change things; and that much was true. Things changed, but not in the way I expected. However, this time I took it seriously. Maybe because I started the process, expecting to be changed. Who knows?

Afterward
(October 2015)

It's close on thirty years now, and it might as well be yesterday. At first glance not that much has changed. Sure Ronald Reagan was rattling the sabre, the Internet and cell phones were in their infancy; and you still had to put film in the camera. From a cultural perspective, that's not much for thirty years. Very little has changed in motorcycle technology either. Compare this to the interval between nineteen twenty through nineteen fifty.

From the perspective of this trip however, one of the changes is significant. I'm not talking about fuel injectors replacing carburetors. Yeah, it would have helped if a pressure sensor in my manifold adjusted the mix in the injector, so I wouldn't need to re-jet the carb at altitude, or dumber yet, pull the air filter.

The smart phone changes everything. Always informed and connected, you'd need to leave it home to recreate the spiritual aspects of this trip - sorry.

Most of this story was written down in 1989, based largely on the journal notes taken during the trip. But surprisingly, I didn't always need them. Unlike many other trips that have blurred over the years, many of these episodes were still fresh in my mind.

Other pieces of the trip were more difficult to reconstruct and there is a good bit of selective compression throughout. I rarely knew the day of the week and was always clueless about the date. As I wrote the journal I assumed it would all be clear, but years later it was anything but. Uneventful days or nights camping just off a road got no mention all, and they've been left out of this story. Even at base camps, some days are combined in the narrative to keep things moving.

'Alone In The Wind' was first typed up on what was a forerunner of today's laptop computer. Failing to obtain a publisher, the text was revised and toyed with for a decade, then forgotten. In 2013, I dusted off the files and started to flesh out the story from a modern perspective. Writing about this trip was a good change of pace from the novel I was writing at the time.

I don't recall why I kept a journal. Writing about trips wasn't something I'd ever contemplated. I was a photographer and at most was thinking about an extended photo essay. In the end, a slide show just never really conveyed the true nature of what I'd experienced.

So this adventure was framed by words, with a few photos added, not so much as art, but as tools to help ground the story and set the stage. A real regret was that I didn't take more pictures of the people I met and spoke with along the way. To some of them I was nothing more than tumbleweed, bouncing through their lives, but with others I made a real connection.

I was (and still am) a photographer. Picture taking consumed the vast majority of my time off the bike. Looking back now, I would have handled it very differently, taking fewer landscapes, and more intensely focused subject shots. But I suppose it's normal to second-guess our own efforts. In the end, the pictures are what they are, and I'm happy to have such complete coverage.

The slides and negatives were stored in boxes, surviving several moves and four kids. I scanned them in 2011 to create digital images, that while lacking the quality of the original format, are more than adequate for the purposes of this document.

The Yamaha is gone as is the Soft Tail that replaced it. I've got my eye on an Indian, but for now I'm on foot; curiosity still insatiable, open to new ideas and experiences, and that's the real ride.

Ghosts In The Wind –
by the best selling author of Alone In The Wind.

The #1 New Release in Adventure Travel

The garage door cranked open as the engine warmed and I stared out at the black hole beyond - the whole of the trip was out there, waiting in the darkness. I pulled on the helmet as my daughter waved goodbye. "When will you come home?"

"I'll be back before the last leaf falls."

For almost eight weeks and 8500 miles, I'd be immersed in American history, geography and culture, following Lewis & Clark to the Pacific, George Custer along Rosebud Creek to the Little Bighorn, exploring the northern lands and working my way to the western sea. There would be time to circle the Great Lakes into Canada, ride the Dakota high prairie, time for Yellowstone, Beartooth Pass, and Mt. St. Helens. I'd roam the Rockies, Bitterroot, Cascades and the Sierra, running down more backroads than I would have thought possible. I had the luxury of getting away alone, immersing myself in the trip, discarding phones & calendars, anything that might distract me from what I was seeing and doing.

Ghosts In The Wind - complete with pictures and maps.

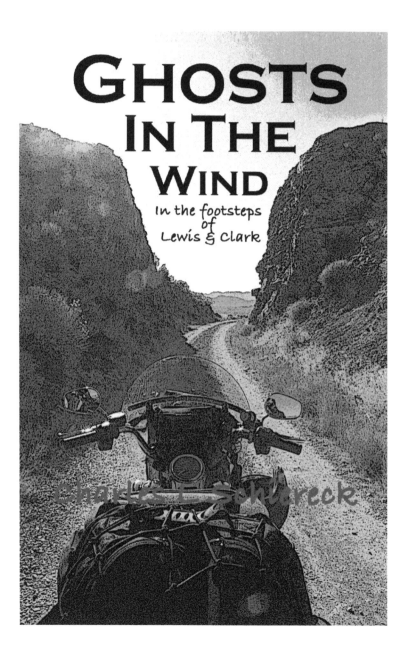

GHOSTS IN THE WIND

In the footsteps of Lewis & Clark

I hope that you've enjoyed
"ALONE IN THE WIND"

Please spare a moment to write a short review on Amazon.

Just go to the Amazon Sales page for "Alone in the Wind – A Journal of Discovery In The Summer of 88", scroll down to the reviews then click the

Write a customer review

button

I enjoy hearing from readers. Email me at author@schiereck.com
I make every effort to reply

Thank you,
Chuck Schiereck

Appendix A: The Pictures
View Them In Color

All of the pictures displayed in the book are black and white versions of the original Kodachrome 64 slides. If you're interested in viewing them in color, they can be found on Face Book Page "Alone In the Wind" By Chuck Schiereck

They are also available on FLICKR.com, at the following link:

https://www.flickr.com/photos/105293353@N07/sets

Or search flickr for 'Chuck chiereck'

Appendix B: STATISTICS

Below is a short list of statistics from the trip. The miles estimated refers to miles logged after the speedometer cable broke on the return leg in Montana.

Bike	1986 Yamaha Virago
Miles logged	10,453
Miles Estimated	1,800
Gas used	224 gallons
AVG. MPG	54
Total Fuel Costs	$240
Avg. $/Gal.	$1.07
States Visited	24
Rolls of Film Used	38

Appendix C: For Those Planning A Similar Trip

Lots of riders have published reams of useful opinion on this topic and I'm not shy about adding to that pile. There are a lot of ways to skin this cat, and there's no 'right way'. If someone speaks on this topic with absolute certainty, my guess is they haven't done very much of it.

The Plan: Have a plan, even a vague one. For the trip discussed in this book, my stated plan was to follow my nose and it doesn't get much more vague than that. If you read this book though, it's clear that there was a skeletal plan and it fleshed out over time, evolving as needed. That's probably true for a lot of people. Some days I wandered, while on others I set up a base camp and tried to get the most out of a given area. Here are some thoughts.

People tour because they love to ride. If you don't, there are more comfortable ways to go. For some, the ride is all they care about. For the rest of us, a plan that balances riding and site seeing is a better bet. Either way, you'll have a fuller experience if you put some effort into a little research.

If you have a few National Parks in your plan, a 'Golden Eagle Pass' is worth the investment. Check it out.

Roads. There's a long-standing gospel opinion that a trip with no interstate highway travel is somehow superior. If you're that insecure, stay home. A wide-open secondary road through scenic terrain is about the best, no argument. However, after crawling along behind RV's for a few days; or easing through cattle on open range; I-90 might look pretty good for a bit. The USA is a big place; a lot of stretches are empty, and they're going to be empty for a long time and a lot of miles. How much of that are you aching to see? For some riders they want to see all of it. That's cool, but I prefer to cherry pick. This isn't 'shortening the trip' if you spend the extra time slogging into a Zion canyon or backcountry at Crater Lake. Balance it out. Do what *you* want and make your own choices, but base them on something real. *There are no rules.*

The Bike. I hear a lot of talk about the best bikes to take. There is no best bike, and the one that most guys take is the one that's already in their garage. Here are some considerations:

I wouldn't recommend air-cooled on a long hot trip again (but I still do it). A lot of that engine heat will be on your legs. An air-cooled, V-twin rear cylinder will struggle to get enough cooling on hot days. If this is your ride, consider an oil cooler and oil temp gauge. If you hate the way that looks, take it off when you get back; or go without one, wear chaps, take breaks and let the engine cool.

Some bike brands have dealers in every small western town. On a long trip, you'll need to be serviced, maybe repaired. Keep it in mind and do your research.

This isn't something you want to be surprised with.

How big the bike needs to be has a lot to do with how big the rider is and their personal preferences. I took an air-cooled cruiser, (750 cc) cross country and back. A medium sized rider, this was fine for me. It was big enough to be comfortable and small enough to get me down some rough dirt tracks.

Out west you'll want a big fuel tank. Extended range is your friend.

A windscreen is a good idea for protecting your face, and reducing fatigue. Many riders prefer to have the wind in their face. Normally that's me, except when touring.

If you're on an old bike with a carb(s), you may want to re-jet them at high altitude. I've pulled the air filter in the past to improve airflow: a dumb idea. A better idea is to ride a fuel-injected bike and not worry about it at all.

Accommodations. If you're staying in hotels, you'll be comfortable.

If you plan on camping, it's a great choice as long as you're prepared to deal with bad weather, the extra work involved, and a lot more baggage. There can be real magic in remote campsites - unforgettable times that won't be happening at the Hilton (my opinion and no disrespect intended). For long trips, consider buying a season pass from a major campground chain. Often they're not overly attractive, but you'll save a good buck, and after doing six hundred miles, you might not care about rustic. Maybe a store, shower, pool and washing machines will be more appealing. You can always grab a hotel if the weather is horrible or you want a break.

Base Camps. This isn't the same as accommodations. There are many places in the USA that can't be appreciated by taking a sniff as you blow through or by just spending a day. Setting up a base camp in a central location, and taking the time to enjoy a region is a great strategy. You won't need to repack the bike every day and riding will be more fun. Base camps can re-energize you when the edges start to fray.

Clothes. It's up to you, but less is more for me. Most people bring too much clothing. Now when I tour, I bring a pair of jeans, t-shirts (long and short sleeved), socks, underwear, polypro, leathers, sneakers, and raingear. There's a lot of noise about bringing raingear, and pretty much of it is just noise. It all boils down to this: *You won't need raingear unless it rains.* Out west in summer, you should be ok without. In the East or Pacific North West, if it rains for a few days, leathers won't keep it out, and they'll be water logged and heavy for a while. If you can cope with being wet for a stretch (without whining) – you're good. If I have space for raingear, I pack it. The last piece of clothing is a pair of nylon shorts to wear when everything else is in the washing machine. You would have figured that out the first time you washed clothes, like I did.

Maps: GPS is great if you've got one. Maps are better for planning tomorrows route, especially if there's a group of people involved.

Camera: If you take your pictures using a phone you'll regret it. Bring a real camera.

Keep a journal. However much info you write, you're going to wish you'd done more.

Sunglasses and glacier glasses if you have them will help with the western sun. Clear eye protection for night driving is a good idea. When I have space, I bring a full-face helmet and I've been glad it was there for hailstorms and frozen mornings. Cold and hot weather gloves: if you don't have them, you'll wish you did.

Dry Runs. If you've never toured before and are planning a long trip, a dry run is a smart move. You'll learn a lot about what works, doesn't work, or isn't needed in the first few days. Do a short one or two night trip and figure it out beforehand. It's better to leave stuff in the garage than in a rest stop trashcan.

Servicing. Get a full service before you head out and reduce your service intervals on the road. I'm not just talking about oil changes. Heat, dust, and long miles take a toll.

Go It Alone? I've done it both ways. Going solo is an unforgettable experience. You go where you want, when you want, without having to debate or bicker over any of it. It might be just what you need if you have an unquenchable wanderlust. You'll pay a price, and if you accept that up front, you'll be ok.

Sharing the trip with someone adds companionship and maybe a few manageable disagreements. However, there will always be someone to share the memories with. Both ways work.

Good Luck.

ACKNOWLEDGMENTS

A sizable group of family, friends and colleagues encouraged, advised and assisted with the trip's considerable logistics including: help in planning a rough itinerary, selecting a bike, and advice on what to bring. There were small gifts to be opened in many of the states, and they meant a lot to a lonely guy when opened at some godforsaken campsite.

Edward Giambalvo and Marsha Auerbach generously gave assistance with every aspect of editing this story.

It goes without saying that a trip of this nature required a significant level of open-mindedness and tolerance from my employer, Mars Incorporated. It was deeply appreciated.

Thank you all.

Manufactured by Amazon.ca
Bolton, ON